S0-BCQ-312

GRADE **8**

McGraw-Hill's
Math

New York   Chicago   San Francisco   Lisbon   London   Madrid   Mexico City
Milan   New Delhi   San Juan   Seoul   Singapore   Sydney   Toronto

The *McGraw-Hill* Companies

Copyright © 2011 by the McGraw-Hill Companies, Inc. All rights reserved. Printed in the United States of America. Except as permitted under the United States Copyright Act of 1976, no part of this publication may be reproduced or distributed in any form or by any means, or stored in a database or retrieval system, without the prior written permission of the publisher.

3 4 5 6 7 8 9 10 11 12 13 14 15 DOW/DOW 1 9 8 7 6 5 4 3 2

ISBN   978-0-07-174861-2
MHID   0-07-174861-X

Editorial Services: SkyBridge Publishing
Production Services: Watch This Space, Inc.
Design Services: PlanetGraham Design

Printed and bound by RR Donnelley.

Cataloging-in-Publication data for this title are on file at the Library of Congress.

McGraw-Hill books are available at special quantity discounts for use as premiums and sales promotions, or for use in corporate training programs. To contact a representative please e-mail us at bulksales@mcgraw-hill.com.

This book is printed on acid-free paper.

Table of Contents

Table of Contents

To the Student

This book is designed to help you master eighth grade mathematics—and gain the confidence to succeed in math as you move on to higher grades. Short lessons explain key points, and exercises help you practice what you have learned. To make the most of your study, follow this 5-step plan:

First, begin with the **Pretest**. This will identify areas where you need additional help, as well as areas where your math knowledge is already strong.

Second, read the **Table of Contents**. Seeing which math topics are covered and the order in which they appear will help guide your work.

Third, check out at the **10-Week Summer Study Plan**. If you have only a limited time, such as summer vacation, to work through this book, this chart will help you plan your study time. Remember, the Study Chart is only a guide for you. You may cover some lessons more quickly, and you may need to spend more time on other lessons.

Fourth, pay particular attention to the hints you'll find when you see the word **Remember**. These will help you remember key points that can make your math work easier.

Fifth, take the **Posttest**. Your results will show you which math topics you've mastered—and whether there are any topics that you need to return to and study again.

Finally, remember the old saying "Practice makes perfect." In mathematics, practice may not guarantee perfection, but it's sure to sharpen your skills, build your confidence, and make you the better math student you want to be.

10-Week Summer Study Plan

Many students will use this book as a summer study program. If that's what you are doing, here is a handy 10-week study plan that can help you make the best use of your time.

When you complete each day's assignment, check it off by marking the box. Each assignment should take you approximately 30 minutes.

	Day	Lesson(s)	Test	✔
Week 1	Monday	1.1, 1.2	Pretest	
	Tuesday	2.1, 2.2		
	Wednesday	3.1, 3.2		
	Thursday	3.3, 3.4		
	Friday	3.5, 3.6		
Week 2	Monday	4.1, 4.2, 4.3		
	Tuesday	4.4, 5.1, 5.2		
	Wednesday	5.3, 5.4		
	Thursday	6.1, 6.2		
	Friday	6.3, 6.4		
Week 3	Monday	6.5, 6.6		
	Tuesday	6.7, 6.8		
	Wednesday	6.9	Lessons 1–6 Unit Test	
	Thursday	7.1, 7.2		
	Friday	7.3, 7.4		
Week 4	Monday	8.1, 8.2		
	Tuesday	9.1, 9.2	Lessons 7–9 Unit Test	
	Wednesday	10.1		
	Thursday	10.2, 10.3		
	Friday	10.4, 10.5		
Week 5	Monday	11.1		
	Tuesday	11.2, 11.3		
	Wednesday	11.4		
	Thursday	12.1, 12.2		
	Friday	12.3	Lessons 10–12 Unit Test	

	Day	Lesson(s)	Test	✔
Week 6	Monday	13.1, 13.2		
	Tuesday	13.3, 13.4		
	Wednesday	14.1		
	Thursday	14.2		
	Friday	14.3	Lessons 13–14 Unit Test	
Week 7	Monday	15.1, 15.2		
	Tuesday	15.3, 15.4		
	Wednesday	15.5, 16.1		
	Thursday	16.2, 16.3		
	Friday	16.4		
Week 8	Monday	17.1, 17.2		
	Tuesday	17.3	Lessons 15–17 Unit Test	
	Wednesday	18.1, 18.2		
	Thursday	19.1, 19.2		
	Friday	19.3		
Week 9	Monday	20.1, 20.2		
	Tuesday	20.3, 21.1		
	Wednesday	21.2, 21.3		
	Thursday	21.4, 22.1		
	Friday	22.2	Lessons 18–22 Unit Test	
Week 10	Monday	23.1, 23.2		
	Tuesday	23.3, 23.4		
	Wednesday	24.1, 24.2		
	Thursday	24.3, 24.4		
	Friday	24.5, 24.6	Lessons 22–24 Unit Test & Posttest	

Pretest

Complete the following test items.

1 Kathy runs 16 miles a week. If she continues to run at this rate, how many miles will she run in a year?

_____

2 The women's clothing department at Ms. Smith's store had a sale on jeans. There were 945 jeans in stock at the beginning of the sale and another 254 jeans were ordered. At the end of the sale the store still had 245 jeans in stock. How many jeans were sold during the sale?

_____

3 Jack has 16 lengths of rope. Each is $6\frac{3}{4}$ meters long. How much rope does Jack have to divide among 20 people?

_____

How much rope will each person receive?

_____

4 David has 176 ounces of hot sauce to divide among the 32 contestants in a chicken-wing eating contest. How many cups is that per contestant?

_____

5 $4\frac{3}{10} + 3\frac{2}{5} + \frac{1}{3} + \frac{1}{2} =$

_____

6 $-8 + 11 - (-9) + 4(-3) + \frac{12}{-4} =$

_____

7 Solve for x: $x - 7 = 14$

_____

8 Solve for x: $2x + 6 = 18$

_____

9 Solve: $10 + (8 - 6)^2 - (12 \div 4) + 5(6 \times 2) + 3(7 - 4) =$ _____

10 Restate in exponent form, then solve: $5 \times 5 + 2 \times 2 \times 2 + 3 \times 3 =$

_____

11 3.55 meters = _____ inches (Use 2.54 cm = 1 inch)

12 10 yards = _____ centimeters

13 What is the area of the rectangle? _____

What is the perimeter?

_____

What is the perimeter, in inches, using the conversion factor of 2.54 cm to the inch?

_____

12 cm
8 cm

14

10 in.
B   A   C

What is the area of the circle? _____
(Use 3.14 for π.)

What is the circumference of the circle?

_____

15 Identify each angle as obtuse, acute, or right.

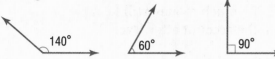

140°   60°   90°

_____ _____ _____

16 Identify each triangle as scalene, isosceles, or equilateral.

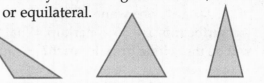

_____ _____ _____

Calculate and reduce the fractions.

17 $4\frac{3}{5} \times 5\frac{1}{5} =$ _____

18 $\left(\frac{3}{4} \times \frac{4}{11}\right) \times \frac{11}{3} =$ _____

19 $\frac{12}{25} \div \frac{4}{5} =$ _____

20 Give the coordinates for points on the grid.

A _____   B _____

C _____   D _____

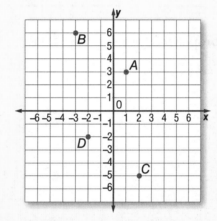

21 What is the measure of angle DBC?

_____

22 $.15\overline{).235}$

23 $3\overline{).4686}$

24 What is 40% of .775? _____

25 What is $\frac{5}{8}$ of 72%? _____

26 Restate 4.25 as an improper fraction and a mixed number.

Improper Fraction _____   Mixed Number _____

27 Put the following numbers in order from least to greatest.
1.162, 1.161, 2.16302, 2.163, 2.8022, 1.90688, 1.9122, 1.099

_____

28 Solve for x. $\frac{15}{32} = \frac{x}{160}$ _____

29 Restate $2\frac{7}{16}$ as a decimal. _____

30 Sarah manufactured surfboards at a cost of $45.00 each. She wants to sell the surfboards at a 50% markup. What will be the selling price for each?

_____

31 Dexter deposits $200 in a bank account that earns 3% simple interest. How much money will he have in the account after 1 year? _____

After 2 years? _____

32 Identify each quadrilateral.

_____ _____ _____ _____ _____

33 Restate $5\frac{6}{13}$ as an improper fraction.

_____

34 Restate $\frac{43}{16}$ as a mixed number. _____

35 $\frac{4}{7} - \frac{5}{7} + \frac{3}{7} + \frac{4}{7} - \frac{3}{7} =$ _____

36 $\frac{5}{8} \times 3\frac{13}{25} =$ _____

37 $10^4 \times 10^5 =$ _____

38 $9^8 \div 9^4 =$ _____

39 What is 12^2? _____

40 What is the square root of 225? _____

41 What is the mode of the data distribution?

_____

What is the median?

_____

$$
\begin{array}{c|l}
2 & 2\ 3 \\
3 & 1\ 6\ 8 \\
4 & 2\ 7\ 7\ 7 \\
5 & 3\ 4\ 4\ 6\ 6 \\
6 & 1\ 4\ 4\ 5
\end{array}
$$

42 According to this graph, what frozen yogurt is the most preferred? _____

The least preferred? _____

43 Brandon collected about 20 cans more than what person? _____
Who collected the second fewest cans? _____

Favorite Flavors of Frozen Yogurt

Recycling Contest

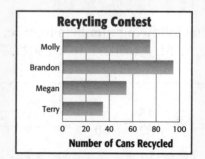

44 How many possible combinations are there?

_____

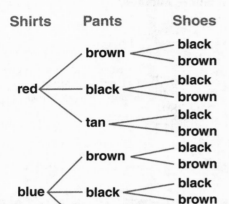

45 What is the range of the data in the box-and-whisker plot?

_____

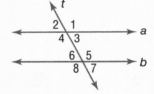

46 Use the Pythagorean Theorem to find the value of x.

_____

47 Name two pairs of alternate interior angles.

_____ and _____   _____ and _____

Name two pairs of alternate exterior angles.

_____ and _____   _____ and _____

Name a pair of vertical angles.

_____ and _____

Name two pairs of supplementary angles.

_____ and _____   _____ and _____

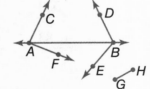

48 Name two line segments. _____

Name four rays. _____

Name a line. _____

Calculate the volume and surface area of the figures shown.

49

50

51

Volume _____

Surface Area _____

Volume _____

Surface Area _____

Volume _____

Adding and Subtracting Whole Numbers

A whole number is a number that does not include decimals or fractions. Most people use *only* whole numbers when they count. Look at these three numbers: $17\frac{3}{4}$, 19.3, and 29. Which one is a **whole number**?

Example:

To add 1372 + 49 + 2891, start by lining up the **addends**, the numbers you have to add, by place value. Add up each place value, *starting in the ones place*. If the total of a place value has 2 digits, write the second digit and **carry** the first digit to the next column.

```
  1 2 1  ← The small numbers in
  1372     the top row represent
    49     numbers that are carried.
+ 2891
  4312
```

Exercises   ADD

1
```
  1
  237
+  55
  292
```

2
```
  533
+ 787
 1320
```

3
```
  621
+ 105
  726
```

4
```
 1130
  131
+  12
 1273
```

5
```
 1322
   65
+  19
 1406
```

6
```
   65
  480
+  58
  603
```

7
```
  578
+  97
  675
```

8
```
 3084
+7917
```

9
```
 6451
+4556
 11007
```

10
```
  413
  533
   73
+  83
 1102
```

11
```
 756089
 423409
+  3478
 1182976
```

12
```
 387051
 112979
+  7352
 507382
```

13 Beatrice works the weekend shift at the local nature park. 325 people visited the park on Saturday morning. During the afternoon, another 455 people visited the nature park. That evening, another 175 people attended. How many people, in total, visited the park on Saturday?

```
 325
 455
,175
 955
```
955

14 Trevor is calculating the batting statistics for his baseball team. They hit 145 homeruns, 117 triples, 612 doubles, and 543 singles. Using these statistics, how many times did Trevor's team hit the ball?

```
 145
 117
 612
 543
1417
```
1417

Adding and Subtracting Whole Numbers (cont.)

Example:

To subtract 2564 from 2723, line up the numbers by place value. Subtract each place value, *starting in the ones place*. Since you cannot subtract 4 ones from 3 ones, you have to regroup. Borrow one ten from the tens place to make the 3 ones into 13 ones. In this example, you also have to borrow one hundred from the hundreds place.

$$\begin{array}{r} {\scriptstyle 11} \\ 6\,\overset{\scriptstyle 1}{\cancel{1}}13 \\ 2723 \\ -\ 2564 \\ \hline 159 \end{array}$$

← The small numbers in the top row represent "regrouping."

Remember...

When you add or subtract whole numbers, line up the numbers by place value. Then treat each place value as its own addition or subtraction problem.

Exercises   SUBTRACT

1
$$\begin{array}{r} 1238 \\ -\ 319 \\ \hline 919 \end{array}$$

2
$$\begin{array}{r} 1311 \\ -\ 418 \\ \hline 893 \end{array}$$

3
$$\begin{array}{r} 7862 \\ -\ 778 \\ \hline 7084 \end{array}$$

4
$$\begin{array}{r} 5556 \\ -\ 3967 \\ \hline 1589 \end{array}$$

5
$$\begin{array}{r} 2015 \\ -\ 977 \\ \hline 1038 \end{array}$$

6
$$\begin{array}{r} 575 \\ -\ 15 \\ \hline 560 \end{array}$$

7
$$\begin{array}{r} 5372 \\ -\ 4184 \\ \hline 1188 \end{array}$$

8
$$\begin{array}{r} 905378 \\ -\ 247489 \\ \hline 657889 \end{array}$$

9
$$\begin{array}{r} 115447 \\ -\ 112385 \\ \hline 3069 \end{array}$$

10
$$\begin{array}{r} 244905 \\ -\ 50339 \\ \hline 194566 \end{array}$$

11
$$\begin{array}{r} 307300 \\ -\ 31008 \\ \hline 276292 \end{array}$$

12
$$\begin{array}{r} 540784 \\ -\ 399099 \\ \hline 141685 \end{array}$$

13 The U.S. Forest Service estimated that last year Williams Canyon was home to 325,000 deciduous trees. This season an insect infestation killed 125,889 trees. How many trees are now left standing?

$$\begin{array}{r} 325000 \\ -\ 125889 \\ \hline 199\,11 \end{array}$$

199/11

14 During a recent hurricane, 1,385 of Oak Island's 3,034 inhabitants evacuated the island by ferry. How many of the inhabitants stayed behind during the storm?

$$\begin{array}{r} 3034 \\ -\ 1385 \\ \hline 1649 \end{array}$$

1649

1.2

Problem Solving

First, make sure to read the entire problem before you begin to work.

Second, identify the problem and the skill required to solve it. (Is it addition or subtraction, or both?)

Third, decide what information is needed to solve the problem. Identify any information that is not needed and ignore it.

Fourth, begin to work the problem.

Fifth, check your answer.

> **Example:** Jason worked 156 hours this month. Marc worked 171. How many more hours did Marc work than Jason?
>
> **Step 1:** What skill is needed? Subtraction
>
> **Step 2:** Subtract Jason's hours from Marc's hours.
>
> **Step 3:** $171 - 156 = 15$
>
> **Step 4:** Marc worked 15 more hours than Jason.

Exercises   SOLVE

1 Christine spent 24 minutes on Monday painting for her art project. She painted for 88 minutes on Tuesday, 45 minutes on Wednesday, and 55 minutes on Friday. How many minutes, in total, did she spend working on her art project?

```
  29
  88
+ 45
  55
 212
```
212 min

2 Carl scored 114,564 points on the first level of his computer game. He scored 113,098 on the second level, and 125,888 on the third level. How many points, in total, did he score on all three levels?

```
 114564
 113098
 125888
 353550
```
353550

3 Jane has 175 stamps in her stamp collection, Stella has 133 stamps in her collection, and their cousin Penny has 212 stamps in hers. If Jane and Stella combine their stamp collections, how many more stamps will they have than Penny?

```
  133
+ 175
  308
- 212
   96
```
96

4 The student council helped organize a jump rope competition for the school. During the competition, Team A jumped the rope 1,339 times in 20 minutes. Team B jumped 1,448 times in 22 minutes, and Team C jumped the rope 1,552 in 23 minutes. What is the total number of times that the students jumped rope?

```
 1339
 1449
 1352
 4339
```
4339

5 Larry spent Saturday afternoon reading his book. If he started the day on page 256, and stopped on page 539, how many pages did he read on Saturday?

```
  539
- 256
  283
```
283

6 The average baby rhinoceros weighs 143 pounds at birth. Fully grown, the average weight of a rhinoceros is 3,950 pounds. How much weight will the average rhinoceros gain in its lifetime?

```
 3950
- 143
 3807
```
3807

Multiplying and Dividing Whole Numbers

MULTIPLICATION Is multiplying whole numbers more difficult than adding or subtracting them?

Not really, if you remember to line up the numbers by place value. Then multiply the *entire* top number by the ones place of the bottom number, and then by the tens place, and then by the hundreds place, and so on for larger numbers. Think of it as doing a few simple problems, one after the other. After you've finished multiplying, add the lines to find the **product**. The product is the answer to the entire multiplication problem.

Example:

$$\begin{array}{r} 356 \\ \times\ 294 \\ \hline 1424 \end{array}\ (4 \times 356)$$
(+) 32040 (90 × 356)
(+) 71200 (200 × 356)
104664

└ placeholder zeroes

Remember...

Always multiply the entire top number by one bottom digit at a time. Use a different line for the product of each bottom digit.

Exercises   MULTIPLY

1
235
× 12
_____
282   *470 2350 7620*

2
332
× 11
_____
3653   *332 3720 3652*

3
177
× 19
_____
3362

4
44
× 130
_____
5720

5
401
× 210
_____
4010 80200 84210

6
509
× 61
_____
509 3054 3563

7
597
× 19
_____

8
618
× 29
_____

9 Ariel earns money by mowing lawns in his neighborhood. If he can mow 3 lawns in an hour, how many lawns can he mow working 30 hours a week?

90

10 Winona is tracking the amount of water that the people of her town use during the summer months. She calculates that 47,005 gallons of water are used every day. If Winona tracks the water usage for 112 days, how much water will be used during that time?

_____

Multiplying and Dividing Whole Numbers (cont.)

DIVISION Is a division problem worked differently from addition, subtraction, and multiplication problems?

Yes. In division, you work from left to right, *not* from right to left! You also have to learn some terms that are used when solving a division problem. The number to be divided is called the **dividend**. The number that goes into the dividend is called the **divisor**. The answer is called the **quotient**, and it shows the number of times the divisor goes into the dividend. The **remainder** is anything left over when you are finished.

Remember...

Your remainder must be *less* than the divisor. If it is not, go back and check your work.

Example:

$$\text{quotient} \longrightarrow 489 \text{ R1} \longleftarrow \text{remainder}$$
$$\text{divisor} \longrightarrow 4\overline{)1957} \longleftarrow \text{dividend}$$
$$\underline{16}$$
$$35$$
$$\underline{32}$$
$$37$$
$$\underline{36}$$
$$1$$

To divide, look at the *highest* place value, the digit at the left of the dividend. Are there any divisors in that number? In this case, the answer is no, there are no 4s in 1. Now look at the *two* highest place values in the dividend. Are there any 4s in 19? Yes, there are 4 of them. Write that number as the first digit of the quotient. Then multiply that number by the divisor and write the product under the dividend. Draw a line, and subtract. Bring down the next digit from the dividend. Repeat that process until you're left with a number that cannot be divided by the divisor.

Exercises **DIVIDE**

1 $8\overline{)1255}$

2 $12\overline{)15289}$

3 $48\overline{)4027}$

4 $9\overline{)1301}$

5 $15\overline{)715}$

6 $12\overline{)403}$

7 $3\overline{)321}$

8 $5\overline{)425}$

9 Aubrey wants to divide his penny collection equally among his 14 cousins. If he has 1,722 pennies in his collection, how many pennies will each one of his cousins receive?

_____

10 Emily wants to bring candy to share with her class at school. If she has 210 pieces of candy, and there are 30 students in her class, how many pieces of candy will each student receive?

_____

Problem Solving

First, make sure to read the entire problem before you begin to work.

Second, identify the problem and the skill required to solve it. (Is it multiplication or division, or both?)

Third, decide what information is needed to solve the problem. Identify information that is not needed and ignore it.

Fourth, begin to work the problem.

Fifth, check your answer.

Example: Bentley picked 252 tomatoes from his 12 tomato plants. On average, how many tomatoes did each plant yield?

Step 1: What skill is needed? Division

Step 2: Divide the number of tomatoes by the number of plants.

Step 3: $252 \div 12 = 21$

Step 4: On average, each plant yielded 21 tomatoes.

Exercises   SOLVE

1 Don volunteers 18 hours a week at the local hospital. If he volunteered 45 weeks last year, how many hours did he spend volunteering?

_____

2 Milos can ride his bicycle an average of 81 miles a day. If he wants to visit his cousin 324 miles away, how many days will it take for him to ride there?

_____

3 Lorraine's cell phone plan allows for 1,200 minutes of free usage every month. During the month of March (March has 31 days), how many minutes a day can Lorraine talk without exceeding her monthly limit?

_____

4 Basil launched his website this year. During the first three months of operation, his site recorded 835,884 hits. If he maintains that same monthly average, how many hits should he expect by the end of the fifteenth month?

_____

5 Camille is counting the number of bricks she needs to build a retaining wall for her herb garden. She calculates that she will need 485 bricks to complete the project. If the bricks come in stacks of 24, how many stacks will she need to complete the project?

_____

6 Iris volunteered to register voters for an upcoming election. She was able to sign up 374 new voters in just 1 voting precinct. If there are 11 precincts in the town, and Iris expects to have the same amount of success in each precinct, how many new voters will she sign up before the election?

_____

Changing Improper Fractions to Mixed Numbers

To understand fractions, there are some terms you need to know. For instance, the number on the bottom is the **denominator**. The denominator tells you what kind of units the whole is divided into: fifths, halves, quarters, and so on. The number on the top is the **numerator**, which tells how many of those units there are.

A fraction is less than 1 when the numerator is less than the denominator. Any fraction greater than 1 is an **improper fraction**. An improper fraction can be changed into a **mixed number**, which is part whole number and part fraction.

Example: Change $\frac{13}{4}$ to a mixed number.

To change an improper fraction into a mixed number, divide the numerator by the denominator. The whole number part is the quotient. The remainder becomes the numerator of the fraction. The denominator remains the same.

Step 1: $13 \div 4 = 3$ with a remainder of 1

Step 2: Write the 3 as your quotient, the 1 as your numerator, and keep the denominator as 4.

$$\frac{13}{4} = 3\frac{1}{4}$$

Exercises   CONVERT TO A MIXED NUMBER

1. $\frac{64}{3}$

2. $\frac{101}{4}$

3. $\frac{15}{2}$

4. $\frac{52}{3}$

5. $\frac{66}{12}$

6. $\frac{137}{11}$

7. $\frac{176}{16}$

8. $\frac{61}{8}$

9. $\frac{121}{21}$

10. $\frac{53}{2}$

11. $\frac{49}{11}$

12. $\frac{312}{19}$

13. $\frac{98}{8}$

14. $\frac{87}{7}$

15. $\frac{159}{12}$

16. $\frac{360}{16}$

17. $\frac{74}{3}$

18. $\frac{71}{4}$

19. Gerrie collects honey from a few beehives. She scoops out the honey with a small jar that holds $\frac{1}{3}$ of a cup. Over the last two weeks Gerrie has filled this jar 158 times. How many cups of honey has she collected?

_____

20. To finish sewing her tapestry, Petra needs 142 strips of cloth that are each one quarter of a yard. How many yards of cloth is that?

_____

Changing Mixed Numbers to Improper Fractions

Now you know how to change an improper fraction to a mixed number. But can you also change a mixed number into an improper fraction? Yes, and it is simple. First, multiply the whole number by the denominator of the fraction. Then, add the numerator to that product. Finally, place the total over the denominator.

Example: Change $8\frac{3}{5}$ into an improper fraction.

Step 1: $5 \times 8 = 40$

Step 2: $40 + 3 = 43$

$$8\frac{3}{5} = \frac{43}{5}$$

Exercises **CONVERT TO AN IMPROPER FRACTION**

1 $5\frac{3}{4}$

2 $7\frac{5}{7}$

3 $25\frac{7}{11}$

4 $24\frac{4}{5}$

5 $16\frac{5}{13}$

6 $14\frac{9}{14}$

7 $53\frac{4}{9}$

8 $17\frac{3}{4}$

9 $3\frac{6}{17}$

10 $62\frac{3}{7}$

11 $22\frac{1}{2}$

12 $32\frac{11}{29}$

13 $27\frac{5}{8}$

14 $25\frac{1}{3}$

15 $41\frac{9}{14}$

16 Gene's bucket holds $\frac{1}{3}$ of a pound of soil. Gene needs to move $10\frac{2}{3}$ pounds of topsoil to his grandmother's garden. How many times will he need to fill his bucket if he wants to move the entire pile of topsoil to the garden?

_____

17 Kayla wants to give a third of a pie to each of her 25 relatives. She has already baked 6 pies. How many more pies will she need to bake so that each relative can have a third?

_____

Name _____

Adding and Subtracting Fractions with Like Denominators

ADDITION Two denominators that are exactly the same are called **like denominators**. They are easy to add, because you ignore the denominators when you add them.

Example: $\frac{5}{9} + \frac{2}{9} = ?$

In this example, all you do is add the numerators. Then place the total over the denominator in both fractions.

Step 1: $5 + 2 = 7$

$$\frac{5}{9} + \frac{2}{9} = \frac{7}{9}$$

Exercises   ADD

1 $\frac{3}{4} + \frac{3}{4}$

2 $\frac{1}{5} + \frac{4}{5}$

3 $\frac{5}{8} + \frac{5}{8}$

4 $\frac{7}{9} + \frac{4}{9}$

5 $\frac{4}{11} + \frac{3}{11}$

6 $\frac{15}{17} + \frac{5}{17}$

7 $\frac{7}{9} + \frac{14}{9}$

8 $\frac{2}{3} + \frac{5}{3}$

9 $\frac{6}{23} + \frac{14}{23}$

10 $\frac{13}{37} + \frac{24}{37}$

11 $\frac{1}{4} + \frac{7}{4}$

12 $\frac{3}{11} + \frac{7}{11}$

13 $\frac{13}{27} + \frac{11}{27}$

14 $\frac{11}{14} + \frac{13}{14}$

15 $\frac{13}{24} + \frac{16}{24}$

16 $\frac{13}{37} + \frac{11}{37}$

17 Manny combined $\frac{1}{7}$ quarts of orange juice, $\frac{2}{7}$ quarts of lemonade, and $\frac{5}{7}$ quarts of raspberry tea into one container. How much liquid is now in the container? Express your answer as a mixed number.

_____

18 James, Riley, and Nancy surveyed their class about the cafeteria food. James surveyed $\frac{2}{9}$ of the class, Riley surveyed another $\frac{5}{9}$ of the class, and Nancy surveyed another $\frac{1}{9}$ of the class. Were the three of them able to poll the entire class?

_____

Adding and Subtracting Fractions with Like Denominators (cont.)

SUBTRACTION Do you use the same process when you subtract fractions with like denominators? Yes, the process is exactly the same! Ignore the denominator when doing your work.

Example: $\dfrac{14}{17} - \dfrac{9}{17} = ?$

Step 1: $14 - 9 = 5$

$\dfrac{14}{17} - \dfrac{9}{17} = \dfrac{5}{17}$

Remember...

To add or subtract fractions with like denominators, you only need to work with the numerators. Then put your total, or difference, over the like denominator.

Exercises   SUBTRACT

1. $\dfrac{3}{4} - \dfrac{1}{4}$

2. $\dfrac{3}{3} - \dfrac{2}{3}$

3. $\dfrac{8}{9} - \dfrac{5}{9}$

4. $\dfrac{7}{8} - \dfrac{1}{8}$

5. $\dfrac{5}{7} - \dfrac{3}{7}$

6. $\dfrac{1}{2} - \dfrac{1}{2}$

7. $\dfrac{2}{3} - \dfrac{1}{3}$

8. $\dfrac{5}{3} - \dfrac{2}{3}$

9. $\dfrac{7}{5} - \dfrac{4}{5}$

10. $\dfrac{4}{7} - \dfrac{1}{7}$

11. $\dfrac{9}{7} - \dfrac{6}{7}$

12. $\dfrac{11}{9} - \dfrac{2}{9}$

13. $\dfrac{6}{5} - \dfrac{3}{5}$

14. $\dfrac{12}{11} - \dfrac{9}{11}$

15. $\dfrac{31}{35} - \dfrac{1}{35}$

16. $\dfrac{21}{22} - \dfrac{17}{22}$

17. Kira made $\dfrac{7}{8}$ quarts of grape juice and served $\dfrac{3}{8}$ quarts for dinner. How much juice does she have left?

_____

18. Ellen bought $\dfrac{19}{16}$ pounds of flour from the store. On her way home, she spilled $\dfrac{11}{16}$ pounds of flour. If she needs $\dfrac{7}{16}$ pounds of flour to make bread, will she have enough flour?

_____

Name _____

Adding or Subtracting Fractions with Unlike Denominators

How do you add or subtract fractions if the denominators are different?

First you have to change the fractions so that they have like denominators. You must find the **common denominator**, another term for like denominator.

Remember...
When you multiply the numerator and the denominator by the same number, the value of the fraction does not change.

Example: $\frac{5}{8} + \frac{1}{6} = ?$

Look at the denominators, 8 and 6. The first thing you have to do is find a number that is a **common multiple** of both numbers. The simplest way to do that is to multiply the two numbers. $8 \times 6 = 48$. There might be a smaller common multiple that is easier to work with. Make a chart of multiples.

	2	3	4
8	16	(24)	32
6	12	18	(24)

When you find the lowest common multiple, take each fraction one at a time. Multiply the original denominator to make it become the common denominator, and multiply the numerator by the same number.

Step 1: Find a common multiple.

Step 2: $\frac{5}{8} = \frac{5 \times 3}{8 \times 3}$

Step 3: $\frac{1}{6} = \frac{4 \times 1}{4 \times 6}$

$$\frac{15}{24} + \frac{4}{24} = \frac{19}{24}$$

Exercises ADD OR SUBTRACT

1. $\frac{3}{4} + \frac{2}{5}$

2. $\frac{5}{7} + \frac{1}{3}$

3. $\frac{11}{20} + \frac{2}{3}$

4. $\frac{1}{4} - \frac{1}{13}$

5. $\frac{1}{4} - \frac{1}{9}$

6. $\frac{2}{21} + \frac{1}{3}$

7. $\frac{34}{11} - \frac{1}{3}$

8. $\frac{11}{7} + \frac{1}{6}$

9. $\frac{11}{15} - \frac{2}{3}$

10. $\frac{5}{8} - \frac{2}{7}$

11. $\frac{14}{11} + \frac{3}{7}$

12. $\frac{11}{12} - \frac{3}{5}$

Adding or Subtracting Mixed Numbers with Unlike Denominators

ADDITION How do you add mixed numbers with unlike denominators?

There are *two* ways to do this. However, in both ways you will first have to find a common denominator for the fractions. One way is to change each mixed number to an improper fraction, then find the common denominator and add the fractions. The other way is even easier. Just add the whole number parts first. Find the common denominator for the fractions and add the fractions. Then add the total fraction to the total of the whole numbers.

Example: $3\frac{2}{3} + 6\frac{1}{2} = ?$

Step 1: Add the whole numbers.
$3 + 6 = 9$

Step 2: Find the common denominator.
$\frac{2}{3} = \frac{4}{6}$ and $\frac{1}{2} = \frac{3}{6}$

Step 3: Add the fractions.
$\frac{4}{6} + \frac{3}{6} = \frac{7}{6} = 1\frac{1}{6}$

$3\frac{2}{3} + 6\frac{1}{2} = 9 + 1\frac{1}{6} = 10\frac{1}{6}$

Remember...

Sometimes, when you add fractions, their total will be an improper fraction. You need to change it to a mixed number before adding it to the total of the whole numbers.

Exercises **ADD**

① $12\frac{1}{2} + 3\frac{3}{4}$

② $13\frac{3}{7} + 4\frac{3}{11}$

③ $5\frac{2}{7} + 3\frac{3}{8}$

④ $3\frac{1}{6} + 7\frac{1}{4}$

⑤ $4\frac{3}{11} + 3\frac{1}{3}$

⑥ $11\frac{1}{2} + 5\frac{2}{5}$

⑦ $4\frac{7}{9} + 5\frac{2}{7}$

⑧ $13\frac{3}{5} + 15\frac{7}{11}$

⑨ $22\frac{5}{6} + 27\frac{5}{13}$

⑩ $1\frac{1}{11} + 7\frac{2}{5}$

⑪ $44\frac{1}{2} + 14\frac{2}{9}$

⑫ $9\frac{5}{7} + 10\frac{1}{3}$

⑬ $4\frac{3}{7} + 4\frac{4}{9}$

⑭ $5\frac{5}{8} + 3\frac{3}{7}$

⑮ $46\frac{4}{7} + 44\frac{1}{2}$

⑯ $4\frac{5}{8} + 3\frac{7}{9}$

Adding or Subtracting Mixed Numbers with Unlike Denominators (cont.)

SUBTRACTION How do you subtract mixed numbers with unlike denominators? First, you need to find a common denominator for the fractions.

Example: $12\frac{5}{7} - 9\frac{2}{5} = ?$

Step 1: $12 - 9 = 3$

Step 2: Find a common multiple for the fraction.

$$\frac{5}{7} = \frac{25}{35} \text{ and } \frac{2}{5} = \frac{14}{35}$$

Step 3: Subtract the fraction.

$$\frac{25}{35} - \frac{14}{35} = \frac{11}{35}$$

Step 4: Add the difference of the whole numbers to the difference of the fractions.

$$3 + \frac{11}{35} = 3\frac{11}{35}$$

What do you do if the second fraction—the one you are supposed to subtract—is *larger* than the first fraction? In this case, subtract the *smaller* fraction from the *larger* fraction. Then, *subtract* the remainder of the fractions from the difference of the whole numbers. The following example will show you how to do this.

Example: $12\frac{5}{7} - 9\frac{4}{5} = ?$

Step 1: $12 - 9 = 3$

Step 2: Find a common multiple for the fraction.

$$\frac{5}{7} = \frac{25}{35} \text{ and } \frac{4}{5} = \frac{28}{35}$$

Step 3: Subtract the smaller fraction from the larger one.

$$\frac{28}{35} - \frac{25}{35} = \frac{3}{35}$$

Step 4: Subtract the fraction from the whole number.

$$3 - \frac{3}{35} = 2\frac{32}{35}$$

$$12\frac{5}{7} - 9\frac{4}{5} = 2\frac{32}{35}$$

Exercises   SUBTRACT

1 $11\frac{5}{9} - 4\frac{9}{13}$ **2** $13\frac{1}{6} - 10\frac{2}{15}$ **3** $15\frac{2}{3} - 14\frac{1}{6}$ **4** $20\frac{3}{4} - 11\frac{4}{9}$

5 $13\frac{5}{6} - 3\frac{5}{7}$ **6** $23\frac{4}{5} - 19\frac{5}{11}$ **7** $13\frac{4}{11} - 3\frac{1}{2}$ **8** $11\frac{2}{3} - 10\frac{7}{9}$

9 $77\frac{1}{3} - 41\frac{5}{17}$ **10** $9\frac{5}{7} - 3\frac{3}{14}$ **11** $31\frac{7}{8} - 12\frac{2}{5}$ **12** $45\frac{1}{3} - 32\frac{3}{7}$

Reducing Fractions

Reducing fractions to their lowest form requires you to divide the numerator and the denominator by a number that divides evenly into both numbers. The way to be certain that you have reduced a fraction correctly is to make sure that there is no number that will divide evenly into both the numerator and denominator. Remember that you will not change the value of a fraction if you multiply or divide its numerator and its denominator by the same number.

Example: Reduce $\frac{48}{120}$ to its lowest form.

Step 1: Find a common factor for both the numerator and the denominator: 12

Step 2: Divide both the numerator and the denominator by that factor:
$48 \div 12 = 4$, $120 \div 12 = 10$

Step 3: Can the numerator and denominator be reduced further? Yes

Step 4: Find another common factor and divide both numbers by that factor:
$4 \div 2 = 2$, $10 \div 2 = 5$
$\frac{2}{5}$ is the lowest you can reduce $\frac{48}{120}$

Exercises   REDUCE

1. $\frac{8}{20}$

2. $\frac{49}{588}$

3. $\frac{525}{1890}$

4. $\frac{168}{3080}$

5. $\frac{24}{150}$

6. $\frac{18}{546}$

7. $\frac{120}{336}$

8. $\frac{220}{650}$

9. $\frac{3}{18}$

10. $\frac{42}{110}$

11. $\frac{3276}{5712}$

12. $\frac{686}{2000}$

13. $\frac{210}{315}$

14. $\frac{66}{528}$

15. $\frac{360}{1650}$

16. $\frac{182}{512}$

4.1

Multiplying Fractions and Whole Numbers

Is there a simple way to multiply a fraction by a whole number? Yes, you multiply the fraction's numerator by the whole number. Then write that product over the fraction's denominator.

Example: $17 \times \frac{2}{3} = ?$

Step 1: Multiply the whole number by the numerator. $17 \times 2 = 34$

Step 2: Place the number in the denominator.
$17 \times \frac{2}{3} = \frac{34}{3}$
If the final fraction is an improper fraction, you need to change it to a mixed number.

Step 3: Convert to a mixed number: $\frac{34}{3} = 11\frac{1}{3}$
$17 \times \frac{2}{3} = 11\frac{1}{3}$

Exercises   MULTIPLY

1 $13 \times \frac{1}{4}$

2 $15 \times \frac{2}{7}$

3 $22 \times \frac{3}{8}$

4 $24 \times \frac{3}{4}$

5 $18 \times \frac{7}{20}$

6 $31 \times \frac{2}{17}$

7 $6 \times \frac{7}{24}$

8 $14 \times \frac{10}{11}$

9 $16 \times \frac{5}{36}$

10 $7 \times \frac{2}{3}$

11 $16 \times \frac{3}{5}$

12 $14 \times \frac{11}{28}$

13 $44 \times \frac{6}{7}$

14 $20 \times \frac{23}{40}$

15 $33 \times \frac{6}{11}$

16 $25 \times \frac{16}{45}$

17 Before setting out on a bike ride, each rider was given $\frac{5}{8}$ gallons of water to carry with them on the trip. If there are 28 people on the bike ride, how much water was dispensed?

_____

18 Norbert estimates that it takes $1\frac{2}{7}$ hours to complete one load of laundry. If Norbert's dad has 8 loads of laundry to do, how long will it take him to finish?

_____

Multiplying Two Fractions; Reciprocals

Is it difficult to multiply two fractions? No, it is simple. Multiply the numerators to get the numerator of the product. Then multiply the denominators to get the denominator of the product.

If the fractions are **reciprocals**, you do not have to multiply at all. Reciprocals are two fractions that look like each other upside-down. The numerator of the first is the denominator of the second and the numerator of the second is the denominator of the first. The product of reciprocals is *always* 1.

Example: $\frac{3}{5} \times \frac{8}{9} = ?$

Step 1: Multiply the numerators. $3 \times 8 = 24$

Step 2: Multiply the denominators. $5 \times 9 = 45$

$$\frac{3}{5} \times \frac{8}{9} = \frac{24}{45}$$

Step 3: Reduce to lowest form. $\frac{24}{45} = \frac{8}{15}$

$$\frac{3}{5} \times \frac{8}{9} = \frac{8}{15}$$

Example: $\frac{2}{3} \times \frac{3}{2} = ?$

Step 1: Multiply the numerators. $2 \times 3 = 6$

Step 2: Multiply the denominators. $3 \times 2 = 6$

$$\frac{2}{3} \times \frac{3}{2} = \frac{6}{6} = 1$$

Exercises   MULTIPLY

1. $\frac{3}{2} \times \frac{4}{9}$

2. $\frac{5}{9} \times \frac{12}{30}$

3. $\frac{15}{21} \times \frac{6}{25}$

4. $\frac{1}{2} \times \frac{1}{2}$

5. $\frac{2}{3} \times \frac{3}{4}$

6. $\frac{5}{4} \times \frac{16}{35}$

7. $\frac{5}{18} \times \frac{9}{25}$

8. $\frac{4}{14} \times \frac{28}{64}$

9. $\frac{13}{22} \times \frac{11}{13}$

10. $\frac{12}{13} \times \frac{52}{72}$

11. $\frac{2}{15} \times \frac{2}{15}$

12. $\frac{21}{24} \times \frac{8}{35}$

13. $\frac{48}{21} \times \frac{42}{64}$

14. $\frac{7}{9} \times \frac{9}{14}$

15. $\frac{15}{18} \times \frac{9}{25}$

16. $\frac{10}{13} \times \frac{26}{45}$

17. Daisy runs on an oval track that is $\frac{1}{4}$ of a mile long. If she runs $\frac{5}{16}$ of the way around the track, how far did she run?

_____

18. Bart's family's motorboat uses $\frac{22}{6}$ gallons of gas every hour. If they run the boat for $\frac{1}{3}$ of an hour, how much gas will they be using?

_____

Name _____

Multiplying Fractions and Mixed Numbers

How do you multiply a fraction and a mixed number? The easiest way is to change the mixed number into an improper fraction. Then multiply the fractions as you would normally.

Remember...

You do not always have to wait until you finish multiplying to reduce. Sometimes you can reduce *before* you multiply. If you are multiplying two fractions, look at both numerators and then at both denominators. If you can divide *either* numerator by the same number as *either* denominator, you can reduce! For example: The denominator 10 and the numerator 15 can both be divided evenly by 5.

$$\frac{17}{10} \times \frac{15}{4} = \frac{17}{(10 \div 5)} \times \frac{(15 \div 5)}{4} = \frac{17}{2} \times \frac{3}{4} = \frac{51}{8}$$

Example: $4\frac{1}{8} \times \frac{1}{3} = ?$

Step 1: Change the mixed number into an improper fraction. $4\frac{1}{8} = \frac{33}{8}$

Step 2: Multiply the fractions. $\frac{33}{8} \times \frac{1}{3} = \frac{33}{24}$

Step 3: Convert the improper fraction to a mixed number and reduce. $\frac{33}{24} = 1\frac{3}{8}$

$$4\frac{1}{8} \times \frac{1}{3} = 1\frac{3}{8}$$

Exercises   MULTIPLY

1 $6\frac{3}{4} \times \frac{1}{9}$

2 $\frac{1}{10} \times 4\frac{1}{6}$

3 $12\frac{1}{4} \times \frac{2}{7}$

4 $3\frac{1}{7} \times \frac{14}{11}$

5 $\frac{2}{5} \times 3\frac{3}{4}$

6 $4\frac{5}{7} \times \frac{7}{11}$

7 $4\frac{2}{5} \times \frac{3}{11}$

8 $3\frac{1}{4} \times \frac{4}{13}$

9 $3\frac{3}{5} \times \frac{10}{9}$

10 $\frac{3}{13} \times 4\frac{1}{3}$

11 $3\frac{2}{3} \times \frac{2}{11}$

12 $5\frac{1}{5} \times \frac{3}{13}$

13 $5\frac{1}{4} \times \frac{1}{3}$

14 $2\frac{4}{5} \times \frac{2}{7}$

15 $2\frac{1}{4} \times \frac{3}{10}$

16 $3\frac{1}{3} \times \frac{3}{5}$

17 Thomas can walk on his hands $20\frac{2}{5}$ yards in a minute. How far can he go in $\frac{3}{4}$ minutes?

18 Peyton plays a round of golf in $3\frac{3}{8}$ hours. How long would it take him to play $\frac{2}{3}$ rounds of golf?

Multiplying Mixed Numbers

You know that mixed numbers can be changed into improper fractions. You also know how to multiply fractions. Can you figure out how to multiply mixed numbers? First you need to change the mixed numbers into improper fractions!

Example: $1\frac{7}{10} \times 3\frac{3}{4} = ?$

Step 1: Convert both mixed numbers into improper fractions. $1\frac{7}{10} = \frac{17}{10}$ and $3\frac{3}{4} = \frac{15}{4}$

Step 2: Multiply the improper fractions and reduce. $\frac{17}{10} \times \frac{15}{4} = \frac{255}{40} = \frac{51}{8}$

Step 3: Convert your fraction to a mixed number. $\frac{51}{8} = 6\frac{3}{8}$

$1\frac{7}{10} \times 3\frac{3}{4} = 6\frac{3}{8}$

Exercises   MULTIPLY

① $5\frac{1}{2} \times 3\frac{3}{4}$

② $2\frac{1}{3} \times 2\frac{4}{5}$

③ $8\frac{1}{5} \times 3\frac{1}{7}$

④ $1\frac{3}{4} \times 12\frac{1}{3}$

⑤ $2\frac{1}{2} \times 4\frac{2}{3}$

⑥ $3\frac{1}{8} \times 3\frac{1}{7}$

⑦ $11\frac{1}{5} \times 6\frac{2}{3}$

⑧ $9\frac{1}{2} \times 5\frac{1}{5}$

⑨ $1\frac{2}{3} \times 7\frac{1}{5}$

⑩ $8\frac{3}{4} \times 3\frac{1}{2}$

⑪ $3\frac{5}{8} \times 5\frac{1}{4}$

⑫ $4\frac{2}{3} \times 4\frac{1}{2}$

⑬ $3\frac{1}{5} \times 2\frac{1}{10}$

⑭ $10\frac{4}{5} \times 2\frac{1}{11}$

⑮ $22\frac{5}{9} \times 1\frac{3}{5}$

⑯ $14\frac{3}{4} \times 2\frac{5}{7}$

5.1

Dividing Fractions by Whole Numbers

Dividing fractions differs from the method you used to divide whole numbers. You actually divide fractions by *multiplying*! To divide a fraction by a whole number, multiply the denominator by the whole number.

Example: $\frac{7}{9} \div 3 = ?$

Step 1: Multiply the denominator by the whole number. $9 \times 3 = 27$

Step 2: Reduce, if necessary.

$$\frac{7}{9} \div 3 = \frac{7}{27}$$

Exercises   DIVIDE

1 $\frac{3}{2} \div 4$

2 $\frac{6}{16} \div 4$

3 $\frac{6}{27} \div 3$

4 $\frac{1}{12} \div 4$

5 $\frac{18}{57} \div 2$

6 $\frac{14}{15} \div 7$

7 $\frac{4}{9} \div 9$

8 $\frac{12}{18} \div 12$

9 $\frac{16}{22} \div 4$

10 $\frac{15}{19} \div 3$

11 $\frac{12}{31} \div 6$

12 $\frac{55}{63} \div 20$

13 $\frac{33}{477} \div 11$

14 $\frac{3}{14} \div 9$

15 $\frac{15}{31} \div 5$

16 $\frac{16}{63} \div 4$

17 Julius receives $\frac{3}{4}$ pounds of Swiss chocolate from his grandmother and wants to divide the chocolate evenly among his 8 friends. How much chocolate will each friend receive?

_____

18 Paola has $\frac{18}{25}$ yard of yarn. She wants to cut the yarn into 3 equal pieces to make button loops. How long should she cut each piece?

_____

Dividing Whole Numbers by Fractions

Dividing a whole number by a fraction also involves multiplication. To divide a whole number by a fraction, you multiply the whole number by the reciprocal of the fraction.

Example: $5 \div \frac{2}{3} = ?$

Step 1: Multiply the whole number by the reciprocal of the fraction. $5 \times \frac{3}{2} = \frac{15}{2}$

Step 2: Reduce, if necessary, and convert to a mixed number. $\frac{15}{2} = 7\frac{1}{2}$

$$5 \div \frac{2}{3} = 7\frac{1}{2}$$

Exercises DIVIDE

1 $5 \div \frac{1}{10}$

2 $9 \div \frac{3}{5}$

3 $14 \div \frac{7}{8}$

4 $12 \div \frac{4}{9}$

5 $12 \div \frac{3}{4}$

6 $42 \div \frac{7}{9}$

7 $45 \div \frac{5}{8}$

8 $24 \div \frac{2}{7}$

9 $16 \div \frac{2}{5}$

10 $5 \div \frac{3}{8}$

11 $16 \div \frac{4}{7}$

12 $39 \div \frac{3}{11}$

13 $15 \div \frac{3}{11}$

14 $14 \div \frac{7}{4}$

15 $27 \div \frac{3}{11}$

16 $33 \div \frac{3}{8}$

17 Brandon worked with his community to provide aid packages for recent hurricane victims. Each package was to contain $\frac{4}{15}$ pounds of sugar. How many packages could Brandon fill if he had 60 pounds of sugar to distribute?

_____

18 Dahlia is planning a bike trip with her friends. Her plan is to ride for $\frac{3}{5}$ hour and then rest for $\frac{1}{5}$ hour. If the entire trip will take 20 hours to complete, how many rest stops will the team make during the ride?

_____

Name _____

Dividing Fractions by Fractions

How do you divide a fraction by another fraction? You multiply the first fraction by the reciprocal of the second.

Example: $\frac{3}{10} \div \frac{2}{3} = ?$

Step 1: Multiple the first fraction by the reciprocal of the second. $\frac{3}{10} \times \frac{3}{2} = \frac{9}{20}$

Step 2: Reduce, if necessary.

$$\frac{3}{10} \div \frac{2}{3} = \frac{9}{20}$$

Exercises   DIVIDE

1 $\frac{6}{7} \div \frac{3}{8}$

2 $\frac{4}{14} \div \frac{2}{16}$

3 $\frac{2}{9} \div \frac{3}{7}$

4 $\frac{1}{4} \div \frac{1}{8}$

5 $\frac{5}{13} \div \frac{5}{9}$

6 $\frac{7}{9} \div \frac{1}{7}$

7 $\frac{1}{13} \div \frac{1}{3}$

8 $\frac{5}{17} \div \frac{2}{17}$

9 $\frac{4}{5} \div \frac{1}{4}$

10 $\frac{15}{24} \div \frac{5}{3}$

11 $\frac{6}{11} \div \frac{11}{7}$

12 $\frac{13}{17} \div \frac{26}{17}$

13 $\frac{3}{11} \div \frac{22}{33}$

14 $\frac{4}{7} \div \frac{4}{21}$

15 $\frac{9}{14} \div \frac{3}{7}$

16 $\frac{3}{5} \div \frac{5}{3}$

17 A recipe calls for the use of $\frac{1}{16}$ ounce of batter for each muffin. How many muffins can be made from $\frac{7}{8}$ ounces of batter?

_____

18 How many miles can a go-cart travel on a full tank of gas if the gas tank holds $\frac{15}{16}$ gallons and burns $\frac{1}{8}$ gallons for each mile traveled?

_____

Name _____

Dividing Mixed Numbers

How can you use a reciprocal to divide one mixed number by another mixed number? First, change both mixed numbers into improper fractions. Then multiply the first fraction by the reciprocal of the second.

Example: $3\frac{3}{5} \div 2\frac{3}{6} = ?$

Step 1: Convert both mixed numbers to improper fractions. $3\frac{3}{5} = \frac{18}{5}$ and $2\frac{3}{6} = \frac{15}{6}$

Step 2: Multiply the first fraction by the reciprocal of the second. $\frac{18}{5} \times \frac{6}{15} = \frac{108}{75}$

Step 3: Reduce, if necessary, and convert to a mixed number. $\frac{108}{75} = \frac{36}{25} = 1\frac{11}{25}$

$3\frac{3}{5} \div 2\frac{3}{6} = 1\frac{11}{25}$

Exercises   DIVIDE

1. $3\frac{1}{6} \div 2\frac{1}{3}$

2. $4\frac{3}{7} \div 3\frac{3}{8}$

3. $5\frac{3}{7} \div 2\frac{2}{3}$

4. $5\frac{2}{9} \div 3\frac{2}{7}$

5. $7\frac{2}{5} \div 3\frac{3}{5}$

6. $4\frac{1}{4} \div 2\frac{3}{7}$

7. $3\frac{4}{9} \div 3\frac{2}{9}$

8. $3\frac{4}{11} \div 5\frac{1}{2}$

9. $4\frac{7}{13} \div 2\frac{2}{3}$

10. $3\frac{7}{13} \div 1\frac{5}{8}$

11. $1\frac{6}{7} \div 2\frac{2}{9}$

12. $3\frac{5}{8} \div 1\frac{7}{8}$

13. $2\frac{4}{7} \div 4\frac{1}{3}$

14. $6\frac{1}{2} \div 2\frac{1}{2}$

15. $7\frac{3}{5} \div 1\frac{4}{5}$

16. $1\frac{2}{9} \div 3\frac{1}{7}$

17. Ursula ran for $1\frac{3}{4}$ hours. If she ran $3\frac{3}{4}$ miles in total, how fast did she run in miles per hour?

_____

18. Mason sorted $14\frac{5}{8}$ pounds of laundry into $2\frac{1}{2}$ loads. How many pounds were in each load?

_____

Lesson 5.4   Dividing Mixed Numbers   29

Name _____

Ratios

What is a ratio? A **ratio**, often expressed as a fraction, compares two numbers.

Examples:

Eight people want equal shares of one pie. You could set up a ratio.

$$\frac{1 \text{ pie}}{8 \text{ people}}$$

When you remove the words, you can see that each person should get $\frac{1}{8}$ of the pie.

You can compare *any* two numbers with a ratio. For example: Shaundra read 5 books last month, and Carmen read 4.

$$\frac{5 \text{ Shaundra books}}{4 \text{ Carmen books}}$$

So the ratio of Shaundra's reading to Carmen's reading was 5:4 (Say "five to four"). You can also express this as a mixed number. Shaundra read $1\frac{1}{4}$ times as many books as Carmen.

Exercises   SOLVE

Indicate (True or False) whether the ratios are equal.

① $\frac{10}{6} = \frac{60}{36}$ _____

② $\frac{4}{6} = \frac{16}{24}$ _____

③ $\frac{13}{26} = \frac{39}{78}$ _____

④ $\frac{11}{5} = \frac{132}{60}$ _____

⑤ $\frac{18}{28} = \frac{27}{42}$ _____

⑥ $\frac{6}{19} = \frac{15}{57}$ _____

⑦ $\frac{27}{52} = \frac{58}{104}$ _____

⑧ $\frac{18}{15} = \frac{12}{10}$ _____

State the ratio as a fraction.

⑨ Paul is making a plaster mixture for his sculpture class. If he mixes 5 ounces of plaster with four ounces of water, what is the ratio of plaster to water?

_____

⑩ Erika's mom separates the laundry into sets. If she puts two sheets and three pillow cases into each set, what is the ratio of pillowcases to sheets?

_____

⑪ Floyd is setting tables for a sports banquet. For each place setting, he puts two forks to the left of the plate and a knife and a spoon to the right of the plate. What is the ratio of forks to knives?

_____

⑫ Jean is making pizza. She adds 4 slices of pepperoni and 3 olives to each slice of pizza. What is the ratio of pepperoni to olives?

_____

What is the ratio of olives to pepperoni?

_____

Proportions and Cross-Multiplying

Do you ever have to use more than one ratio to solve a problem? Yes, a **proportion** is a problem that contains two ratios that are equal.

Example:

Suppose you want to give a party for 20 people. You know that two quarts of potato salad will feed 10 people, but how much potato salad will you need if you are feeding 20 people? When you have two ratios, but don't know the value of one of the numerators or one of the denominators, set up a proportion problem. This kind of problem is called an **equation**, a mathematical statement that two things are equal. You can use q to stand for the unknown number of *quarts*.

$$\frac{2 \text{ quarts}}{10 \text{ people}} = \frac{q}{20 \text{ people}}$$

Cross-multiplying is the way to find the missing number. Multiply the numerator of the first fraction by the denominator of the second fraction and write that on one side of the equation. Then multiply the denominator of the first fraction by the numerator of

the second fraction and write that on the other side of the equation. To get the answer, look at the side of the equation that has both a known number and the unknown number. Divide *both* sides of the equation by that known number.

Step 1: Set up your equation. $\frac{2}{10} = \frac{q}{20}$

Step 2: Cross multiply. $2 \times 20 = 10 \times q$

Step 3: Find the side of the equation with the unknown number. Then look at the known number on that side. (In this equation, it's 10.) Divide *both* sides of the equation by that known number. $40 \div 10 = 4$

$$q = 4$$

You will need four quarts of potato salad for 20 people!

Exercises   SOLVE

Indicate (True or False) whether the ratios are equal.

1 $\frac{4}{9} = \frac{36}{81}$ _____

2 $\frac{5}{7} = \frac{35}{42}$ _____

3 $\frac{4}{3} = \frac{12}{9}$ _____

4 $\frac{9}{8} = \frac{16}{18}$ _____

5 $\frac{5}{12} = \frac{125}{300}$ _____

6 $\frac{6}{5} = \frac{36}{32}$ _____

7 $\frac{7}{11} = \frac{84}{132}$ _____

8 $\frac{5}{8} = \frac{25}{40}$ _____

Solve for the unknown variable.

9 $\frac{10}{6} = \frac{n}{36}$

10 $\frac{4}{x} = \frac{16}{24}$

11 $\frac{13}{26} = \frac{y}{78}$

12 $\frac{11}{m} = \frac{132}{60}$

13 $\frac{18}{28} = \frac{n}{42}$

14 $\frac{x}{19} = \frac{15}{57}$

15 $\frac{x}{52} = \frac{58}{104}$

16 $\frac{18}{15} = \frac{n}{10}$

6.3

Rates

A **rate** is a fixed ratio between two things. It is solved exactly like a proportion problem.

> **Example:** Maria drives at a rate of 65 miles per hour. How many hours does it take her to drive 195 miles?
>
> **Step 1:** Express the proportion problem using two ratios. In this problem, let's use h for the unknown number of hours.
>
> $$\frac{1 \text{ hour}}{65 \text{ miles}} = \frac{h \text{ hours}}{195 \text{ miles}}$$
>
> **Step 2:** Cross multiply.
> $$195 = 65 \times h$$
>
> **Step 3:** Divide each side by 65 to solve for h:
> $$h = \frac{195}{65}$$
> $$h = 3$$
>
> So it will take Maria 3 hours to drive 195 miles!

Exercises   SOLVE

1 George likes to sweeten his ice tea. When he is drinking a 20-ounce ice tea, he adds two teaspoons of sugar. If he makes a gallon of ice tea, how many teaspoons of sugar should he add (there are 128 ounces in a gallon)?

_____

2 Peter wants to make scrambled eggs for the customers at the diner. His recipe calls for 12 eggs and is enough for 5 people. How many eggs will he need if he has to feed 75 customers?

_____

3 A person needs to drink 3 quarts of water for every hour of running time. If a runner plans to complete a marathon in 5 hours, how many quarts of water should she drink during the race?

_____

4 Diane's car uses 5 gallons of gasoline to travel 125 miles. How far will Diane be able to travel on 20 gallons of gasoline?

_____

5 When Frank goes on a 4-day vacation with his family, he packs 4 t-shirts and 3 pairs of shorts. If he is going on an extended vacation for 12 days, how many t-shirts and shorts will he need to pack?

_____

6 There were 90 customers at the restaurant on Friday, 60 of whom ordered the vegetarian meal. If there are 195 customers on Sunday, how many vegetarian meals would you expect to sell?

_____

Proportions and Percent

What if you wanted to answer the question, "What percent of 80 is 48?"

Remember that the word percent means "per 100". Think of percent as a proportion where the denominator is always 100. So if you wanted to know what percent 48 is of 80, then you would set the problem up as a proportion.

Examples: What percent of 80 is 48?

Step 1: Express the problem using two ratios. Use x for the unknown. "48 is to 80 as x is to 100" or $\frac{48}{80} = \frac{x}{100}$

Step 2: Cross multiply: $4800 = 80x$

Step 3: Divide each side by 80 to solve for x:
$4800 \div 80 = 60$
$x = 60$
So 48 is 60% of 80.

What if you wanted to know what number is 50% of 90? Just like the first example, you would solve the problem using two ratios.

Step 1: Set up the problem using two ratios. Remember that percent is just a ratio with 100 as the denominator: $\frac{x}{90} = \frac{50}{100}$

Step 2: Cross multiply: $100x = 4500$

Step 3: Divide each side by 100: $4500 \div 100 = 45$
$x = 45$
So 45 is 50% of 90.

Exercises   CALCULATE USING PROPORTIONS

1. 40% of 50 is _____

2. 72 is 18% of _____

3. 14 is _____% of 35

4. 12% of 85 is _____

5. 50 is 40% of _____

6. 18 is _____% of 270

7. 70% of 70 is _____

8. 66 is 30% of _____

9. 1.5 is _____% of 75

10. 140% of 95 is _____

11. 13 is 65% of _____

12. 12 is _____% of 32

6.5

Percent Change, Mark-up, and Discount

When calculating **percent change**, you are determining the percentage change from a starting point. If you want to determine the percent your height has changed, say from 65 inches to 70 inches, you want to know how much it has changed relative to your starting height of 65 inches. Simple subtraction tells us your height has changed 5 inches, but to calculate the percent change, you must set up an equation: $\dfrac{\text{Change}}{\text{starting point}} = \dfrac{x}{100}$

Example:

Starting height = 65 inches
Change in height = (70 in. − 65 in.) = 5 inches

Step 1: Set up your equation: $\dfrac{5}{65} = \dfrac{x}{100}$

Step 2: Calculate: $500 = 65x$ $7.69 = x$
Your height has increased approximately 7.69%

Mark-up is an amount that you want to add to something you sell. Say your store's headquarters has determined that you should sell all your products at cost plus 25%; the 25% is called the mark-up. One way to calculate

mark-up is to take the cost, calculate 25% of the cost, and add it to the cost. This is your selling price. If you have a product that costs $200, what is the mark-up and selling price? To calculate the mark-up you must set up a proportion.

Example:

Step 1: Set up your equation: $\dfrac{x}{200} = \dfrac{25}{100}$

Step 2: Calculate: $100x = 5000$ $x = 50$
Your mark-up is $50, so you would sell the product for $200 + $50 = $250

Discount is much like a mark-up, but instead of increasing the price, you are reducing the price of an item. You are at a sale and the sign states to take 30% off all items. You see an MP3 player that has a price of $150. How much is it after the discount?

Example:

Step 1: Set up your equation: $\dfrac{x}{150} = \dfrac{3}{100}$

Step 2: Calculate: $100x = 4500$ $x = 45$
The discount is $45, so the sale price would be $150 − $45 = $105

Exercises SOLVE

1 What is the selling price for an item that costs $50 and has a mark-up of 40%?

_____

2 What is the mark-up amount for an item that costs $125 and has a mark-up of 35%?

_____

3 What is the selling price for an item that costs $70 and has a discount of 40%

_____

4 What is the discount amount for an item that costs $160 and has a discount of 45%?

_____

Percents and Fractions

Can you express percents in ways other than as a decimal? Yes, you can change percents into fractions. The denominator of a percent is *always* 100, and the numerator will be the number of the percent.

Example: 30% of 50 = ?

Step 1: Convert the percent to a fraction:
$$30\% = \frac{30}{100}$$

Step 2: Simplify the fraction if you can:
$$\frac{30}{100} = \frac{3}{10}$$

Step 3: Multiply: $\frac{3}{10} \times 50 = \frac{150}{10}$

Step 4: Simplify the product: $\frac{150}{10} = 15$
So 30% of 50 = 15

Some fractions can be turned into simple percents. If the denominator of the fraction can divide evenly into 100, find the quotient. Then multiply the numerator by the quotient, and add the percent sign. If the denominator of the fraction cannot divide evenly into 100, the fraction *cannot* be converted into a simple percent.

Example: $\frac{2}{5} = ?\%$

Step 1: Divide 100 by the denominator:
$$100 \div 5 = 20$$

Step 2 Multiply the numerator by the product:
$$2 \times 20 = 40$$

Step 3: Add the percent sign. 40%
So $\frac{2}{5} = 40\%$

Exercises   CALCULATE USING MULTIPLICATION

1 18 is _____% of 60

2 20% of 85 is _____

3 $\frac{42}{70}$ = _____%

4 30% of 90 is _____

5 $\frac{16}{128}$ = _____%

6 $\frac{12}{48}$ = _____%

7 15% of 60 is _____

8 $\frac{24}{160}$ = _____%

9 35% of 220 is _____

10 $1\frac{1}{5}$ = _____%

11 40% of 65 is _____

12 $\frac{75}{250}$ = _____%

13 $\frac{3}{50}$ = _____%

14 $\frac{55}{1100}$ = _____%

15 65% of 40 is _____

Name _____

Multiplying Percents and Fractions

Can you multiply percents and fractions? Of course! You've learned that percents can be expressed as fractions. So just convert the percent to a fraction and multiply the two fractions. But remember these two important points:

• If you find a percent of a fraction, the product will be a fraction.

• If you find a fraction of a percent, the product will be a percent.

Example: What is 50% of $\frac{2}{3}$?

Step 1: Convert the percent to a fraction:
$50\% = \frac{1}{2}$

Step 2: Multiply the fractions: $\frac{1}{2} \times \frac{2}{3} = \frac{1}{3}$
50% of $\frac{2}{3}$ is $\frac{1}{3}$

Example: What is $\frac{1}{6}$ of 96%?

Step 1: Convert the percent to a fraction:
$96\% = \frac{96}{100}$

Step 2: Multiply the fractions:
$\frac{1}{6} \times \frac{96}{100} = \frac{96}{600} = \frac{16}{100}$

Step 3: Convert back to a percent:
$\frac{16}{100} = 16\%$

Another way to find a fraction of a percent is to multiply the percent, *as if it were a whole number*, by the fraction. The product will almost always be an improper fraction. Change that fraction into a mixed number and add the percent sign.

Exercises CALCULATE

1 $\frac{5}{12} \times 60\% =$ _____

2 $\frac{3}{5} \times 82\% =$ _____

3 $\frac{6}{5} \times 55\% =$ _____

4 $\frac{8}{25} \times 125\% =$ _____

5 $\frac{4}{15} \times 75\% =$ _____

6 25% of $\frac{4}{5} =$ _____

7 20% of $\frac{5}{6} =$ _____

8 40% of $\frac{15}{16} =$ _____

9 75% of $\frac{112}{150} =$ _____

10 60% of $\frac{40}{75} =$ _____

11 $\frac{7}{12} \times 72\% =$ _____

12 $\frac{5}{4} \times 42\% =$ _____

Percents and Decimals

How can you convert decimals with thousandths, ten thousandths, and even smaller places into percents? Just move the decimal point two places to the right and then add the percent sign.

Example: Rename .46072 as a percent.

.46072 = 46.072%

Exercises   CONVERT

Convert to a percent.

1 .7612

_____

2 .01543

_____

3 1.59

_____

4 .5721

_____

5 .0012

_____

6 .000134

_____

7 10.45

_____

8 1.89

_____

9 .569

_____

10 .9999

_____

11 0.0011

_____

12 3.1345

_____

13 99.99

_____

14 .175555578

_____

15 .187

_____

16 .87

_____

Simple and Compound Interest

SIMPLE INTEREST What does *simple interest* mean when you're talking about a loan or a bank account? How do you calculate it? The amount you borrow or put into the bank is called the **principal**. Simple interest is a percent of the principal that has to be paid, by you, if you borrow money, or by the bank, to you, if you deposited money. The **interest** is money that is *added* to the principal.

Example: Principal = $500
Rate of Interest for one year = 4%

Step 1: Interest (i) =
Principal (p) × Rate of Interest (r):
$500 × 4% = i

Step 2: Convert the Rate of Interest to a fraction:
$4\% = \dfrac{4}{100}$

Step 3: Calculate: $500 × \dfrac{4}{100} = 20.00

If you wanted to pay the loan back at the end of the year, you would have to pay both the principal and the interest.

$p + i =$
$500 (the principal) + $20 (the interest) = $520

If you deposited this money into a savings account, the bank would have to add $20.00 interest to your deposit at the end of a year.

Exercises   CALCULATE

1 How much interest would you earn if you put $500 in a bank for 15 years and received simple interest of 8%?

_____

2 Calculate the simple interest on a bank account where you deposit $500 and earn 12% a year for 5 years.

_____

3 Calculate the ending balance of your savings account if you deposit $400 and earn simple interest of 7% for 5 years.

_____

4 Calculate the ending balance of your savings account if you deposited $1,000 and earned simple interest of 6% for 6 years.

_____

Simple and Compound Interest (cont.)

COMPOUND INTEREST What is the difference between compound and simple interest? Compound interest pays interest on the principal *and* the interest, while simple interest pays interest only on the principal.

Examples:

	Bank A	Bank B
Starting Balance	$100	$100
Interest Earned Year 1	$10	$10
Ending Balance Year 1	$110	$110
Interest Earned Year 2	$11 ($110 × 10%)	$10 ($100 × 10%)
Ending Balance Year 2	$121	$120
Interest Earned Year 3	$12.10 ($121 × 10%)	$10 ($100 × 10%)
Ending Balance Year 3	$133.10	$130

Let's look at an example where you put $100 in Bank A that pays compound interest of 10% each year, and $100 in Bank B that pays simple interest of 10% each year. We will examine what happens over 3 years.

The difference in balances is due to compound interest. If you want to calculate the balance you will have after *n* years, the formula is:

Starting Balance x (1 + interest rate as a decimal)$^{\text{[to the }n\text{th power]}}$

Calculate the balance at Bank A after 3 years at a compounded interest rate of 10%.

Step 1: Convert the interest rate to a decimal:
10% = .1

Step 2: Set up an equation: $100 x $(1 + .1)^3 = x$

Step 3: Calculate: $100 x $(1 + .1)^3 = 133.10
The balance at Bank A after 3 years is $133.10

Exercises **CALCULATE**

5 Calculate the interest earned over a 5-year period when you deposit $2,000 and earn compound interest of 8% per year.

_____

6 How much interest would you earn if you put $500 in a bank for 20 years and received a compound interest rate of 4%?

_____

7 How much money would you owe if you borrowed $2,000 for 5 years, with a compound interest rate of 28%, and did not make any payments during that period?

_____

8 Is it better to receive compounded interest for 7 years at 12% on your balance of $500, or to receive the same rate of simple interest for 9 years on that same balance?

_____

Unit Test

Lessons 1–6

Solve.

1 Edie's local newspaper has 4,476 pages of advertising each year. If the magazine is published once a week, about how many pages of advertising are in each issue? (Calculate using 52 weeks in a year.)

_____

How many pages exactly?

_____

Add or subtract.

2
$$\begin{array}{r} 16284 \\ 24768 \\ + 554 \\ \hline \end{array}$$

3
$$\begin{array}{r} 215578 \\ + 20559 \\ \hline \end{array}$$

4
$$\begin{array}{r} 802453 \\ 708109 \\ + 1129 \\ \hline \end{array}$$

5
$$\begin{array}{r} 487 \\ - 294 \\ \hline \end{array}$$

6
$$\begin{array}{r} 1765 \\ - 376 \\ \hline \end{array}$$

7
$$\begin{array}{r} 458581 \\ - 338472 \\ \hline \end{array}$$

8
$$\begin{array}{r} 122977 \\ - 31192 \\ \hline \end{array}$$

9 $\dfrac{31}{4} + \dfrac{3}{4}$

10 $\dfrac{19}{43} - \dfrac{13}{43}$

11 $4\dfrac{5}{11} + 5\dfrac{6}{11}$

12 $2\dfrac{23}{39} + \dfrac{24}{39}$

13 $\dfrac{12}{61} - \dfrac{3}{61}$

Change each to a mixed number.

14 $\dfrac{45}{7}$

15 $\dfrac{66}{8}$

16 $\dfrac{1}{2} \times 44$

17 $\dfrac{1}{4} \times 22$

18 $\dfrac{11}{18} \times \dfrac{11}{22}$

19 $\dfrac{2}{3} \times 4\dfrac{3}{5}$

20 $18 \times \dfrac{7}{9}$

21 $\dfrac{15}{29} \div 45$

22 $\dfrac{54}{47} \div 18$

23 $42 \div \dfrac{7}{3}$

24 $\dfrac{4}{27} \div 3$

25 $\dfrac{75}{83} \div 15$

Unit Test

Lessons 1–6

Determine if the following proportions are equal. (Write Yes or No.)

26 $\dfrac{5}{4} = \dfrac{24}{26}$ _____

27 $\dfrac{21}{12} = \dfrac{7}{36}$ _____

28 $\dfrac{12}{19} = \dfrac{38}{48}$ _____

29 $\dfrac{1}{4} = \dfrac{6}{24}$ _____

Solve for *x*.

30 $\dfrac{x}{10} = \dfrac{30}{20}$

31 $\dfrac{20}{x} = \dfrac{40}{100}$

32 $\dfrac{36}{90} = \dfrac{12}{x}$

Solve.

33 Walter looked at the list of nutrients in the fruit juice he bought. He noticed that there were a total of 4 grams of carbohydrates and 3 grams of sugar in every bottle of juice. Compare the amount of sugar to carbohydrates in the fruit juice.

_____

34 Will rides his unicycle at an average speed of 8 miles per hour. How far will he travel in $2\dfrac{1}{2}$ hours? _____

35 Jack makes 22 muffins for every 3 batches he bakes. How many batches of muffins will he need to bake in order to sell 242 muffins?

_____

36 Priscilla drinks an average of $\dfrac{2}{3}$ quart of water for each mile she walks. How many quarts of water will she drink if she walks $\dfrac{2}{3}$ miles?

_____

37 Jenny changes the oil in her car every 2,250 miles. How many times will she need to change the oil in her car if she takes a trip that is 9,000 miles in length?

_____

Lessons 1-6

38 30% of $1\frac{2}{5}$ **39** 40% of 440   **40** $\frac{1}{4}$ of 48%   **41** $\frac{2}{5}$ of 70%

42 $\frac{3}{8}$ of 340%   **43** 43% of .705   **44** 84% of 1.906   **45** $\frac{3}{4}$ of 160%

46 Pete's Pet Emporium is having a sale on birdcages. Pete is selling his $50 cages at a 20% discount, his $75 cages at $\frac{1}{3}$ off, and his $100 cages at 60% off the original price. What are the new sale prices for the 3 cages?

$50 cage _____ $75 cage _____ $100 cage _____

47 Tom is selling wristbands for $4.50. He has to charge sales tax of 6% on each wristband. What is the cost to the customer, including sales tax, for one wristband?

_____

48 Ursula put $200 into a money market account which pays 3% simple interest. How much will she have in her account at the end of 1 year if she does not deposit any more money in the account?

_____

How much will she have at the end of 2 years?

_____

49 Pam put $400 into a savings account that pays 2.5% in compound interest. How much will she have in the account at the end of 2 years, if she does not deposit any more money in the account?

_____

How much will she have at the end of 5 years?

_____

Place Value and Rounding

Understanding place value can help you work with decimals.

Tens	Ones		Tenths	Hundredths	Thousandths
1	5	.	4	0	7

Look at the chart. Suppose you are asked to round a decimal to its highest whole number. You can do that by looking at the digit in the tenths place. If that digit is less than 5, round down and keep the whole number that is already there. If the digit in the tenths place is 5 or greater, add 1 to the whole number.

You can also round a decimal to its nearest tenth, its nearest hundredth, its nearest thousandth, and so on. Just look at the digit to the *right* of the rounding place. If that digit is less than 5, keep the digit you see in the rounding place. If that digit is 5 or greater, add 1 to the digit in the rounding place.

Exercises ROUND

Round to the nearest whole number.

1 48.6

2 98.3

3 156.67

4 3026.92

5 189.41233

6 2244.66795

7 279.99556

8 428.5

Round to the nearest tenth.

9 124.5755

10 175.5133

11 349.49888

12 313.35664

13 375.77454

14 44.00913

15 566.9943

16 61.15

Round to the nearest hundredth.

17 1536.3357

18 32.4589

19 118.9977

20 523.75776

21 1099.989877

22 1.11881

23 33.43718

24 555.555

Round to the nearest thousandth.

25 729.239788

26 409.13391

27 8056.708035

28 549.594959

29 99.80007

30 177.555901

31 2012.20507

32 901.901445

Name _____

Changing Fractions to Decimals

What is the difference between a decimal and a fraction?

Actually, a decimal *is* a fraction expressed in a different way.

So $0.7 = \frac{7}{10}$ and $5.023 = 5\frac{23}{1000}$

However, decimals are expressed only in tenths, hundredths, thousandths, and so on. So some fractions cannot be converted to simple decimals.

Example: $\frac{5}{8} = ?$

Every fraction represents its numerator divided by its denominator. So $\frac{5}{8} = 5 \div 8$. Set up a simple division problem. Add a decimal point and as many placeholder zeros as you need in your dividend.

$$
\begin{array}{r}
.625 \\
8{\overline{\smash{\big)}\,5.000}} \\
\underline{4.8} \\
20 \\
\underline{16} \\
40 \\
\underline{40} \\
0
\end{array}
$$

As you can see,
$\frac{5}{8} = .625$, or six hundred twenty-five thousandths.

Exercises CONVERT TO DECIMAL

Round to the nearest thousandth.

① $1\frac{5}{16}$ ② $2\frac{4}{7}$ ③ $\frac{48}{200}$ ④ $3\frac{375}{500}$ ⑤ $\frac{6}{202}$

⑥ $7\frac{13}{33}$ ⑦ $\frac{52}{156}$ ⑧ $4\frac{11}{15}$ ⑨ $1\frac{1}{2001}$ ⑩ $2\frac{33}{78}$

⑪ $2\frac{15}{32}$ ⑫ $2\frac{45}{76}$ ⑬ $4\frac{13}{45}$ ⑭ $\frac{17}{18}$ ⑮ $5\frac{7}{16}$

⑯ $4\frac{13}{19}$ ⑰ $2\frac{7}{10000}$ ⑱ $\frac{7}{250}$ ⑲ $1\frac{97}{103}$ ⑳ $3\frac{7}{11}$

Changing Decimals to Fractions

Can you also change decimals to fractions? Yes, and it is much easier to do than changing fractions into decimals. Begin by looking at the *place value* farthest to the right. Use that as your denominator. The decimal number becomes the numerator. After you have changed the decimal into a fraction, you might even be able to reduce it.

Example: $.72 = \dfrac{72}{100} = \dfrac{18}{25}$

Exercises   CONVERT TO FRACTION

1 1.3 _____

2 .60 _____

3 .588 _____

4 3.875 _____

5 6.75 _____

6 1.125 _____

7 3.26 _____

8 .625 _____

9 4.2 _____

10 12.101 _____

11 2.009 _____

12 .3125 _____

13 1.046875 _____

14 2.64 _____

15 5.55 _____

16 22.222 _____

17 5.8 _____

18 33.99 _____

19 3.5 _____

20 8.18 _____

21 Chad had .625 gallons of gas left in his lawnmower at the end of summer. Restate the amount as a fraction.

_____

22 Wanda toured the milk processing plant with her class. The guide said there were over .75 miles of conveyor belts in the plant. Restate that number as a fraction.

_____

Comparing and Ordering Decimals

If you look at place values, you can compare and order decimals just as you can compare and order whole numbers. Remember to line up your decimals so that the decimal points are all in the same column. As with whole numbers, each digit is one place value *higher* than the digit to its immediate right.

When comparing whole numbers with decimals, always look at the whole numbers first. If two whole numbers are the same, *then* compare by moving right from the decimal point. To compare decimals like .07 and .072, you can imagine a placeholder zero to make them both fill the same number of places. So .07 = .070. That is less than .072!

Example:
Order these decimals:
5.62   6.186   0.2   .07   5.65   .071   .009

Decimals: 5.62
6.186
0.2
.07
5.65
.071
.009

The order, reading from greatest to least is:
6.186, 5.65, 5.62, 0.2, .071, .07, .009

Remember...

When comparing numbers with decimals, always look at the whole numbers first. If two whole numbers are the same, then compare the numbers *to the right* of the decimal point.

Exercises   **COMPARE**

Order from least to greatest.

1 1.3, 1.031, 1.322, 13.1, .1332, 1.5, 1.55, 1.505

_____

2 .751, .75, 7.51, .705, .075, .34, 1.675, 1.68

_____

3 .17, 1.7, .017, .00175, .01695, .107, 1.07

_____

4 .45, .625, .405, .420, .415, .451, 1.4

_____

Order from greatest to least.

5 .25, .333, .15, .155, .125, .33

_____

6 .332, .3334, .334, .3, .3033, .0335, 1.0001

_____

7 .6667, .7501, .6, .75, .751, .707, .667

_____

8 .68, .55, .6, .63, .6665, .06665, .59996

_____

Adding Decimals

Is there anything special you need to know in order to add decimals? Yes, you need to make sure to line up your addends by place value. Once you do that, adding decimals is *exactly* the same as adding whole numbers.

Example: 79.46 + 8.65

$$\begin{array}{r} 79.46 \\ +\ 8.65 \\ \hline 88.11 \end{array}$$

Remember...

You also need to put a decimal point in its proper column in the total!

Exercises   ADD

1
$$\begin{array}{r} 145.415 \\ 22.1 \\ +\ .4667 \\ \hline \end{array}$$

2
$$\begin{array}{r} 436.911 \\ +\ 401.22 \\ \hline \end{array}$$

3
$$\begin{array}{r} 57.477 \\ 81.534 \\ +\ .000543 \\ \hline \end{array}$$

4
$$\begin{array}{r} 12.232 \\ 3.001 \\ +\ 5.0019 \\ \hline \end{array}$$

5
$$\begin{array}{r} 73.045 \\ .011 \\ +\ 3.1 \\ \hline \end{array}$$

6
$$\begin{array}{r} 11.0809 \\ +\ 13.2291 \\ \hline \end{array}$$

7
$$\begin{array}{r} .882 \\ 15.6 \\ +\ .466 \\ \hline \end{array}$$

8
$$\begin{array}{r} 44.32 \\ +\ 2.1109 \\ \hline \end{array}$$

9
$$\begin{array}{r} 6.5 \\ 3.5001 \\ +\ .334 \\ \hline \end{array}$$

10
$$\begin{array}{r} 33.154 \\ 4.46 \\ +\ .004 \\ \hline \end{array}$$

11
$$\begin{array}{r} 5.9201 \\ +\ 7.383 \\ \hline \end{array}$$

12
$$\begin{array}{r} .704 \\ 19.0007 \\ +\ .0056 \\ \hline \end{array}$$

13
$$\begin{array}{r} 4.248 \\ 5.774 \\ +\ 333.707 \\ \hline \end{array}$$

14
$$\begin{array}{r} 9.465 \\ +\ 55.7287 \\ \hline \end{array}$$

15
$$\begin{array}{r} .00852 \\ +\ 12.1549 \\ \hline \end{array}$$

16
$$\begin{array}{r} .242 \\ +\ 3.7031 \\ \hline \end{array}$$

17 Troy plays for the football team as a punter. Last week Troy made three punts of 11.324 meters, 12.6742 meters, and 10.227 meters. What was the total length of these three punts?

_____

18 Kate measured the amount of rain that fell during the last three rainstorms. She measured .903 inches of rainfall for the first storm, 1.6778 inches for the second storm, and 1.2655 inches for the third storm. What was the total rainfall for the three storms?

_____

8.2

Subtracting Decimals

Is subtracting decimals similar to subtracting whole numbers? Yes, but you have to remember to line up the decimals. Insert placeholder zeros if necessary.

Example: 243 − 178.861

```
  243.000
− 178.861
─────────
   64.139
```

Remember...

The value of a number does *not* change if you add a decimal point at the end and insert placeholder zeros. You can use as many placeholder zeros as you need to complete your calculations.

Exercises   SUBTRACT

1
```
  17.382
−  5.4445
```

2
```
  28.001
− 15.5628
```

3
```
  102.87
−   2.4801
```

4
```
  38.3102
− 33.5305
```

5
```
  13.3333
−  7.777
```

6
```
  19.1113
−  5.3741
```

7
```
  575.002
− 112.3145
```

8
```
  9.0701
− 6.90941
```

9
```
  5.3564
− 4.6881
```

10
```
  14.1507
−  5.20404
```

11
```
  69.7055
− 63.64
```

12
```
  3.532
− 2.7829
```

13
```
  179.312
−  55.155
```

14
```
  9.651
− 6.9118
```

15
```
  5.87
− 3.899
```

16
```
  263.741
−   8.81
```

17 The winner of the pole vault recorded a best vault of 5.8833 meters. The second place winner recorded a best vault of 5.4993 meters. What was the difference between the winning vault and the second-place vault?

_____

18 Annie measured the depth of the water in the school's fountain and found there were 9.774 inches of water. Annie measured the depth of the water again the next day and noted that the water level was 1.7456 inches lower. What was the new depth of the water?

_____

Multiplying with Decimals

When multiplying decimals, you do *not* line up the decimal points. You just multiply as if there were no decimal points at all. When you are finished multiplying, count the total number of decimal places in the **factors**, the numbers you have multiplied. Then, starting from the right of your product, count that number of places, and put your decimal point to the *left* of the last place you counted.

Example: $33.2 \times .46$

$$
\begin{array}{r}
332 \\
\times\ 46 \\
\hline
1992 \\
13280 \\
\hline
15.272
\end{array}
$$

Exercises   MULTIPLY

1 $\begin{array}{r} 189 \\ \times\ 2.53 \end{array}$ **2** $\begin{array}{r} 7.18 \\ \times\ 2.431 \end{array}$ **3** $\begin{array}{r} 15 \\ \times\ 4.175 \end{array}$ **4** $\begin{array}{r} 1.7 \\ \times\ 7.023 \end{array}$

5 $\begin{array}{r} 77 \\ \times\ 7.770 \end{array}$ **6** $\begin{array}{r} 15 \\ \times\ 2.42 \end{array}$ **7** $\begin{array}{r} 16 \\ \times\ 9.1 \end{array}$ **8** $\begin{array}{r} 55 \\ \times\ 6.333 \end{array}$

9 $\begin{array}{r} 654 \\ \times\ 23.1 \end{array}$ **10** $\begin{array}{r} 96 \\ \times\ 8.8 \end{array}$ **11** $\begin{array}{r} 22.5 \\ \times\ 1.5 \end{array}$ **12** $\begin{array}{r} 5.6 \\ \times\ 2.3 \end{array}$

13 $\begin{array}{r} 6.52 \\ \times\ 63 \end{array}$ **14** $\begin{array}{r} 89.3133 \\ \times\ 63 \end{array}$ **15** $\begin{array}{r} 11.1531 \\ \times\ 32 \end{array}$ **16** $\begin{array}{r} 84.176 \\ \times\ 1.54 \end{array}$

17 Pauline's mom drives the soccer team to and from each of their away games. If the team has 12 away games, and on average Pauline's mom uses 2.775 gallons of gas to make the round trip, how much gas will she use for the whole season?

_____

18 The delivery truck driver has 64 packages to deliver to the school. The average weight of a package is 13.7552 pounds. If the delivery truck has a load capacity of 900 pounds, can the delivery driver deliver all 64 packages in one load?

_____

Name _____

Dividing with Decimals

When dividing a decimal by a whole number, *only* the dividend has a decimal point. To calculate correctly, you must line up a decimal point in the quotient with the decimal point in the dividend.

When dividing either a decimal or a whole number by a decimal, you must move the decimal point of the divisor all the way to the right. So you must multiply the divisor by whatever power of 10 will do that. Then, you have to also multiply the dividend by that same power of 10.

Examples:

92.4 ÷ 7

Step 1: Complete the division problem, and make sure the decimal in the quotient aligns with the decimal in the dividend:

```
      13.2
   7)92.4
      7
      22
      21
       14
       14
        0
```

27 ÷ .08

Step 1: Multiply both numbers by 100:
.08 × 100 = 8   27 × 100 = 2700

Step 2: Complete the division problem:

```
       337.5
   8)2700.0
     24
      30
      24
       60
       56
        40
        40
         0
```

Exercises   DIVIDE

① 4.51)335

② 7.1)416

③ 7.71)214

④ 8.8)172

⑤ 3.7)239

⑥ 6.11)44.8

⑦ 5.8)55

⑧ 7.8)254

⑨ 4.09)281

⑩ 3.52)156

⑪ 12.1)102.201

⑫ 24)91.91

Unit Test

Lessons 7–9

Round to the nearest tenth.

1 3406.997

2 334,782.099

3 65,529.0887

_____   _____   _____

Round to the nearest hundredth.   **Round to the nearest ten thousandth.**

4 2,467,891.3554   **5** 97.009   **6** 17.99986   **7** 99.11115

_____   _____   _____   _____

Identify the place value of the underlined number.

8 1,683,679.573<u>4</u>4 _____

9 1,499,667.5<u>7</u>73 _____

Convert the decimal to a fraction.

10 .8 = _____

11 .875 = _____

12 .08 = _____

Convert the fraction to a decimal.

13 $\frac{3}{5}$ = _____

14 $\frac{8}{15}$ = _____

15 $\frac{3}{16}$ = _____

Put the decimals in order from least to greatest.

16 .122, .1145, .616, .6165, .513, .3132, .2126, .819

_____

17 .217, .0217, .0133, .0487, .1243, .20413, .5257, .05257, .05205

_____

Unit Test

Name _____

Lessons 7–9

Add or Subtract.

18
```
  1.157397
+ 2.31542
```

19
```
  3.10341056
+ 3.431776
```

20
```
  1.1564
  2.1667
+ 3.337833
```

21
```
  4.15466
- 2.2355
```

22
```
  1.892754
- .464043
```

23
```
  2.4276
- .17813344
```

24
```
  $1.25
+ $5.5
```

25
```
  $1.89
+ $ .89
```

Multiply or Divide.

26
```
  .4033
×   90
```

27
```
  14.615
×   145
```

28
```
25)$2.67
```

29
```
  4.539
× 1.65
```

30
```
  $1.64
×   56
```

31
```
  1.7965
× 1.657
```

32
```
  $15.00
× .1575
```

33
```
24)35.487
```

34
```
2.24)14.293
```

35
```
.23)2.69
```

36
```
.025).5805
```

37
```
  .4033
× .95
```

38
```
  15.615
×   15
```

39
```
15)$3.75
```

40
```
  4.589
× 1.45
```

41
```
  $1.58
× .65
```

Lessons 7–9

42 Chad and his service club collected a total of 954.75 pounds of canned food for the local animal shelter. There are 15 people in the club. If each member collected the same amount of canned food, how many pounds did each member collect?

_____ pounds

43 Jane went to the store to buy food for a party of 6 neighbors. For each guest, she spent $2.55 for salad, $1.75 for a cold beverage, and $1.25 for a fruit cup. How much did she spend in total to buy the food?

_____

Jane has $35. Does she have enough money to buy everything she needs?

_____

If so, then how much change will Jane get back?

_____

44 Rodney runs on a cross-country course that is 2.35 miles in length. During the week he ran the course $5\frac{1}{2}$ times. How far did he run that week?

_____

45 Stan is preparing pots for planting flowers. He has 23.5 pounds of potting soil. If Stan fills each pot with 1.35 pounds of potting soil, how many pots can he fill?

_____

46 Billy charges 45¢ per square foot to varnish patio decks. If the patio deck he is varnishing is 220.25 square feet in area, how much should Billy charge for the job?

_____

47 Tracy mixed cold beverages for all of the teams participating in a local baseball tournament. For each batch, she mixed 3.25 gallons of lemonade with 1.3 gallons of iced tea. If Tracy made $8\frac{3}{4}$ batches, how many gallons of cold beverage did she make?

_____ gallons

Multiplying and Dividing Exponents

What if you want to multiply $3 \times 3 \times 3$? Or $5 \times 5 \times 5 \times 5$? Is there a simple way you can write that?

Yes, you can use an **exponent**. The number you keep multiplying by itself is called the **base**. The exponent (written as a small number next to and slightly above the base) tells how many times you multiply the base by itself.

Example: exponent

2^4 3^5 9^2 10^3

$2^4 = 2 \times 2 \times 2 \times 2 = 16$

$3^5 = 3 \times 3 \times 3 \times 3 \times 3 = 243$

$9^2 = 9 \times 9 = 81$

$10^3 = 10 \times 10 \times 10 = 1000$

Exponents are also called **powers**. So 10^3 is 10 to the third power. Any number can be a base. For example, 64 is 4 to the third power.

Often, when a base is raised to the second power, we use the word "squared." 25^2 can be expressed as "25 to the second power," or "25 squared." When a base is raised to the third power, we often use the word "cubed." So 12^3 can be expressed as "12 cubed."

Is there a simple way to multiply and divide bases that have exponents?

Yes. Can you figure out how to do that by looking at the following information?

$$3^2 \times 3^3 = 3^5 \qquad 2^4 \times 2^7 = 2^{11}$$
$$4^6 \div 4^4 = 4^2 \qquad 10^7 \div 10^3 = 10^4$$

Can you see how to do it?

To multiply a base raised to a power by the *same* base raised to a power, simply add the exponents. To divide a base raised to a power by the same base raised to a power, simply subtract the exponents.

Exercises   CALCULATE

Express your answer using a base and an exponent.

1 $4^5 \times 4^5$

2 $7^5 \div 7^3$

3 $3^{16} \div 3^4$

4 $12^{22} \times 12^5$

5 $11^7 \times 11^5$

6 $12^{32} \div 12^{10}$

7 $10^5 \times 10^4$

8 $23^7 \div 23^6$

9 $16^{16} \div 16^2$

10 $15^5 \div 15^3$

11 $11^{11} \div 11^2$

12 $4^4 \times 4^7$

Powers

What if you have a problem with 2 exponents separated by parentheses? Is there a rule for how to calculate that expression? Yes, let's take a look at the example.

What about an expression that looks like $(A^m)^n$, except the parentheses are left out: A^{m^n}?

In this case, the order of operations says that you calculate exponents first, so it would be A raised to the m^n power.

So $53^{3^3} = 5^{27}$

> **Example:** $(5^3)^3$
>
> This expression means 5^3 multiplied by itself 3 times.
>
> $(5 \times 5 \times 5) \times (5 \times 5 \times 5) \times (5 \times 5 \times 5) = 5^9$
>
> The rule for this type of exponential expression is:
> $(A^m)^n = A^{m \times n}$

Exercises   CALCULATE

Express your answer using a base and an exponent.

1 $(5^4)^3$

5^{12}

2 $(8^7)^5$

8^{35}

3 $(14^{10})^7$

14^{70}

4 $(3^{20})^8$

3^{160}

5 7^{6^4}

7^{24}

6 8^{2^4}

8^8

7 19^{8^3}

19^{24}

8 15^{9^3}

15^{27}

9 $(8^3)^8$

8^{24}

10 $(2^5)^6$

2^{30}

11 $(7^4)^{15}$

7^{60}

12 $(13^5)^3$

13^{15}

13 18^{2^8}

18^{16}

14 277^{6^4}

277^{24}

15 $(33^3)^{15}$

33^{45}

16 $(3^4)^5$

3^{20}

More about Exponents

All the work that you have done with exponents has been with a positive number as the exponent, but there are also negative exponents.

What number does 5^{-3} represent? If we multiply $5^3 \times 5^{-3}$ and use the properties of exponents that you already learned, then $5^3 \times 5^{-3} = 5^{3+(-3)} = 5^0 = 1$

5^{-3} is the multiplicative inverse of 5^3, so $5^{-3} = \dfrac{1}{5^3} = \dfrac{1}{125}$

When you encounter a negative exponent, you simply apply the same rules of exponents you already know:

$A^m \times A^{-n} = A^{m-n}$

Exercises   CALCULATE

Convert to a fraction.

1 4^{-3}

2 3^{-3}

3 6^{-4}

4 5^{-5}

5 7^{-2}

6 4^{-1}

7 9^{-5}

8 2^{-8}

Convert to exponential form.

9 $\dfrac{1}{64}$

10 $\dfrac{1}{81}$

11 $\dfrac{1}{9}$

12 $\dfrac{1}{25}$

Multiply.

13 $4^4 \times 4^{-2}$

14 $5^7 \times 5^{-4}$

15 $7^{12} \times 7^{-6}$

16 $14^{24} \times 14^{-20}$

Squares and Square Roots

To square a number means that you take the number and multiply it by itself. If you square 6, the result is 36. This would be written as $6^2 = 36$.

Numbers that result from squaring an integer are called a **perfect square**. The numbers that are perfect squares and less than 200 are: 1, 4, 9, 16, 25, 36, 49, 64, 81, 100, 121, 144, 169, 196.

The **square root** of a number is the number that, when multiplied by itself, is equal to that number. The square root of 196, written

as $\sqrt{196} = 14$ as $14^2 = 196$. The $\sqrt{}$ is called the **radical sign**.

What about the integers that are between the perfect squares? We know that their square roots are not integers. The number 45 is not a perfect square, but you know that its square root must be greater than 6 and less than 7 but closer to 7 as $6^2 = 36$ and $7^2 = 49$. The square root of a number that is not a perfect square is an **irrational number**.

Exercises   CALCULATE

Identify the square root.

1 $\sqrt{49}$ **2** $\sqrt{121}$ **3** $\sqrt{225}$ **4** $\sqrt{81}$

5 $\sqrt{144}$ **6** $\sqrt{4}$ **7** $\sqrt{1}$ **8** $\sqrt{169}$

Estimate the square root of a number.

9 $\sqrt{89}$ is between _____ and _____ but closer to _____

10 $\sqrt{44}$ is between _____ and _____ but closer to _____

11 $\sqrt{5}$ is between _____ and _____ but closer to _____

12 $\sqrt{50}$ is between _____ and _____ but closer to _____

13 $\sqrt{97}$ is between _____ and _____ but closer to _____

14 $\sqrt{23}$ is between _____ and _____ but closer to _____

10.5

Scientific Notation

Is it difficult to write and read long numbers like 4,500,000,000 or 61,020,000? Is there a simpler way to express long numbers? Yes, you could use **scientific notation**, a way to express any number as a product of 10 and a decimal greater than 1.

Examples:

$4,500,000,000 = 4.5 \times 10^9$

$61,020,000 = 6.102 \times 10^7$

When you use scientific notation, notice that the decimal is always *greater than 1*, but *less than 10*. You might think the difficult part is figuring out which power of 10 to use. However, that is not so hard. Look at the number in standard, or regular, notation. Imagine that there is a decimal point to the right of that number. Move the decimal point to the left, one place value at a time, counting each time you move it. *Stop* when your number is greater than 1 but less than 10. Your count is the power of 10.

Exercises   CONVERT

Write each number using scientific notation.

1 .0013

2 810.114

3 4.0095

4 .00005

5 .5851

6 220.467

7 426.7

8 11901.55

9 .0606544

10 .8852

11 1488.951

12 200001.990

13 .0006660

14 .002679

15 1.1110

16 3007.5

Write each number in standard form.

17 2.6699×10^5

18 1.4455×10^3

19 9.6603171×10^6

20 3.0302×10^4

21 2.77×10^{-3}

22 3.919181×10^5

23 1.588×10^3

24 1.0801×10^{-2}

58   Lesson 10.5   **Scientific Notation**

Order of Operations

What happens if you see a long string of mathematical calculations to perform? Is there some way to know where to begin? Yes, you can use a rule called the **order of operations**. It tells you in what order you should do calculations for equations in a long string.

There is even a simple word that can help you remember the order of operations: **PEMDAS**. This stands for **P**arentheses, **E**xponents, **M**ultiplication, **D**ivision, **A**ddition, and **S**ubtraction.

Example:

Solve: $20 - 5 \times 2 + 36 \div 3^2 - (9 - 2) = ?$

We can solve this problem using the order of operations. Remember PEMDAS.

1. Parentheses $(9 - 2) = 7$

   $20 - 5 \times 2 + 36 \div 3^2 - 7 = ?$

2. Exponents $3^2 = 9$

   $20 - 5 \times 2 + 36 \div 9 - 7 = ?$

3. Multiplication and Division $5 \times 2 = 10$

   $36 \div 9 = 4$

   $20 - 10 + 4 - 7 = ?$

4. Addition and Subtraction $20 - 10 = 10$

   $10 + 4 = 14$

   $14 - 7 = 7$

Exercises   CALCULATE

1 $(5 + 2) \times (5 - 3) - (3 \times 3) + 2^{(5-2)}$

2 $(6 - 5) \times (6 - 4) - 2^3 + 6$

3 $(7 - 4)^3 + (7 - 2)^2 + 5 - 2 + 3^{(5-3)}$

4 $(8 + 2) \times (8 - 5) + 42 - (7 - 4)^3$

5 $(8 - 6)^3 - (7 - 5)^3 + 9 - (5 - 2)$

6 $(4)^2 - (2^3 - 5) + (2^2 + 2) - 2^3$

7 $(7 - 2) + (8 - 5) - (4 - 1) - 2$

8 $(4 + 3) \times (5 - 2) \times (2 - 1)^2$

Name _____

Commutative and Associative Properties

Numbers behave in specific ways. Each kind of number behavior is called a property.

Commutative Property of Addition: You can add addends *in any order* without changing the sum. $7 + 3 + 6 = 6 + 3 + 7$

Commutative Property of Multiplication: You can multiply factors *in any order* without changing the product. $5 \times 2 \times 9 = 9 \times 5 \times 2$

Associative Property of Addition: You can group addends any way you like without changing the sum. $(7 + 8) + 3 = 7 + (8 + 3)$

Associative Property of Multiplication: You can group factors any way you like without changing the product. $(3 \times 12) \times 4 = 3 \times (12 \times 4)$

Exercises   IDENTIFY

Identify which property is represented in the example (Commutative or Associative).

1 $8 \times 4 \times 3 = 3 \times 4 \times 8$

_____

2 $(2 + 9) + 22 = 2 + (9 + 22)$

_____

3 $3 \times 4 + 4 \times 2 = 4 \times 3 + 2 \times 4$

_____

4 $4 \times 2 + 3 \times 4 = 3 \times 4 + 4 \times 2$

_____

5 $3 + 2 + 4 = 4 + 2 + 3$

_____

6 $12 + (7 + 1) = (12 + 7) + 1$

_____

7 $(2 + (8 + 6) + 4) = (2 + 8) + (6 + 4)$

_____

8 $6 \times 4 \times 2 = 2 \times 4 \times 6$

_____

9 $(8 + 2) + 9 + 14 = 8 + (2 + 9) + 14$

_____

10 $9 \times 4 + 27 + 4 \times 9 = 4 \times 9 + 27 + 9 \times 4$

_____

11 $7 + 9 + 6 + 4 = 4 + 6 + 9 + 7$

_____

12 $(9 + 9) + 6 + 9 = 9 + (9 + 6) + 9$

_____

13 $29 + 2 + 1 + 29 = 2 + 1 + 29 + 29$

_____

14 $28 + 20 + 28 + 20 = 20 + 20 + 28 + 28$

_____

Distributive and Identity Properties

Distributive Property of Multiplication: To multiply a sum of two or more numbers, you can multiply by each number separately, and then *add* the products. To multiply the difference of two numbers, multiply separately and *subtract* the products.

Some numbers in a problem do not affect the answer. These numbers are called **Identity Elements**.

With adding, the identity element is 0, because any addend or addends + 0 will not change the total. In multiplication, the identity element is 1, because any factor or factors × 1 will not

change the product. However, subtraction and division do not have identity elements.

Examples:

$9 \times (2 + 5) = (9 \times 2) + (9 \times 5)$
$5 \times (12 - 10) = (5 \times 12) - (5 \times 10)$

You can also use the Distributive Property for dividing, but *only* if the numbers you are adding or subtracting are in the dividend.
$(28 + 8) \div 4 = (28 \div 4) + (8 \div 4)$

However, you *cannot* use the Distributive Property when the numbers you are adding or subtracting are in the divisor.
$28 \div (4 + 2)$ *does not* $= (28 \div 4) + (28 \div 2)$

Exercises   IDENTIFY THE PROPERTY

1 $0 + 6 = 6$

_____

2 $4(4 + 1) = 4 \times 4 + 4 \times 1$

_____

3 $7 + 0 = 7$

_____

4 $9 \times 12 + 9 \times 9 = 9(12 + 9)$

_____

5 $4(1 + 1) = 4(1) + 4(1)$

_____

6 $15 + (4 + 0) = 15 + 4$

_____

7 $4(11 + 9) = 4 \times 11 + 9 \times 4$

_____

8 $6 \times 5 + 0 = 6 \times 5$

_____

9 $(34 \times 0) + (7 \times 0) = 0(34 + 7)$

_____

10 $(35 - 1) + (3 - 3 + 0) = (35 - 1) + (3 - 3)$

_____

Rewrite the equation using the distributive property.

11 $4(5 + 7)$

_____

12 $6 \times 2 + 8 \times 2$

_____

Properties of Equality and Zero

Zero Property of Multiplication: Any number multiplied by zero will be zero. $16 \times 0 = 0$

Equality Property of Addition: You can keep an equation equal if you add *the same number* to both sides. $(6 + 4) + 3 = (9 + 1) + 3$

Equality Property of Subtraction: You can keep an equation equal if you subtract *the same number* from both sides.
$(6 + 4) - 5 = (9 + 1) - 5$

Equality Property of Multiplication: You can keep an equation equal if you multiply both sides by *the same number.* $(6 + 4) \times 10 = (9 + 1) \times 10$

Equality Property of Division: You can keep an equation equal if you divide both sides by *the same number.* $(6 + 4) \div 2 = (9 + 1) \div 2$

Remember...

You may **never** divide a number by zero.

Exercises   SOLVE

1 5×0

2 $(2 + 4)\, 0$

3 0×3.56

4 $2\, (5 - 5)$

Identify which Equality Property is being displayed.

5 If $8 + 1 = 6 + 3$, then $4\, (8 + 1) = 4\, (6 + 3)$? _____

6 If $3 \times 15 = 9 \times 5$, then $6 + 3 \times 15 = 6 + 9 \times 5$? _____

7 If $\dfrac{1}{5} = \dfrac{3}{15}$, then $\dfrac{1}{5} - 5 = \dfrac{3}{15} - 5$? _____

8 If $6 \times 7 = 21 \times 2$, then $\dfrac{(6 \times 7)}{4} = \dfrac{(21 \times 2)}{4}$? _____

9 If $3 \times .75 = 2 \times 1.125$, then $\dfrac{(3 \times .75)}{200} = \dfrac{(2 \times 1.125)}{200}$ _____

10 If $20 - 3 = 12 + 5$, then $20 - 3 + 11.5 = 12 + 5 + 11.5$? _____

11 If $3 + 4 + 1 = 11 - 3$, then $3 + 4 + 1 + 8 = 11 - 3 + 8$? _____

12 If $5 - 1 = 20 \times .2$ then does $\dfrac{(5 - 1)}{22} = \dfrac{(20 \times .2)}{22}$? _____

Negative Numbers

Negative numbers are numbers that are less than zero. You identify them by adding a minus sign to the front of a number. So −1 is 1 less than 0. −53.5 is 53.5 less than 0. There are special symbols used in comparing the number value parts.

< means "less than"
> means "greater than"
≤ means "less than or equal to"
≥ means "greater than or equal to"
= means "equal to"

Remember...

Zero (0) is neither positive nor negative.

Examples:

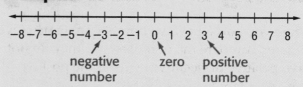

Look at the number line. Notice that −3 is three spaces to the left of 0 on the negative side. Also note that 3 is three spaces to the right of 0, on the positive side.

The Property of Additive Inverses: When you add a negative number to its inverse (its exact opposite on the other side of the number line), the total is 0.

For example, −7 + 7 = 0.

Exercises **CALCULATE**

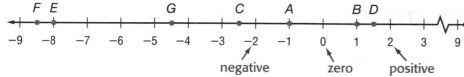

1 On the number line, place and label the number values as points on the number line.
A (−1), B (1), C (−2.5), D (1.5), E (−8), F (−8.5), G (−4.5)
Then order values from least to greatest.

_____

2 Order the number values from greatest to least.
4.6, −6.6, −6, −6.7, −4.3, 3, 3.3, −3.3, 8, −8.1

_____

Use > (is greater than), < (is less than) or = (is equal to) in comparing the number value pairs.

3 −4.5 _____ 4.5

4 −3.3 _____ −3.0

5 7.5 _____ −7.5

6 −7.5 _____ 1.5

7 −6.1 _____ −6.25

8 −5 _____ −4.95

9 13.9 _____ 13.9

10 −9 _____ 9

11 −8 _____ −.888

12.2

Name _____

Adding and Subtracting Negative Numbers

When you add a positive number and a negative number, compare the numbers as if they do not have positive or negative signs. If the positive number is larger, just subtract.

Example: $6 + (-4) = ?$

Step 1: Remove the $+$ sign and the parentheses.

Step 2: Subtract: $6 - 4 = 2$

If the negative number is larger, subtract the smaller number from the larger one. Then put a minus sign in front of the difference.

Example: $1 + (-3) = ?$

Step 1: Subtract the smaller from the greater number: $3 - 1 = 2$

Step 2: Write a minus sign in front of the difference: $1 + (-3) = -2$

When adding two negative numbers, ignore the minus sign and add. Then write a minus sign in front of the total.

Example: $(-1) + (-6) = ?$

Step 1: Ignore the minus signs and add: $1 + 6 = 7$

Step 2: Write a minus sign in front of the total: $(-1) + (-6) = -7$

Exercises   ADD OR SUBTRACT

1 $171 + (-32) =$ _____

2 $(-145) + 61 =$ _____

3 $111 + (-112) =$ _____

4 $715 + (-316) =$ _____

5 $1101 + (-561) - 114 =$ _____

6 $295 + (-365) + (-111) =$ _____

7 $(-210) + (-210) - 427 =$ _____

8 $71 + (-53) + 10 =$ _____

9 $301 + (-222) =$ _____

10 $118 - 181 - (-128) =$ _____

11 $(-125) + 214 =$ _____

12 $85 - 19 + 24 + (-110) =$ _____

13 $27 + (-79) - 30 =$ _____

14 $(-213) + 163 + (-119) =$ _____

15 $42 + 22 + (-67) - (-31) =$ _____

16 $12 - (-29) - 29 =$ _____

Multiplying and Dividing Negative Numbers

Negative numbers can also be multiplied and divided. You just need to remember these two rules:

When two numbers have the same sign, either negative or positive, their product, or quotient, is *positive*.

When two numbers have different signs, one negative and one positive, their product, or quotient, is *negative*.

Examples:

$5 \times 4 = 20$	$(-5) \times (-4) = 20$
$(-5) \times 4 = -20$	$5 \times (-4) = -20$
$6 \div 2 = 3$	$(-6) \div (-2) = 3$
$(-6) \div 2 = -3$	$6 \div (-2) = -3$

Exercises   MULTIPLY OR DIVIDE

1 $-5 \times (-3) =$ _____

2 $15 \times (-10) =$ _____

3 $-100 \div 12 =$ _____

4 $-25 \times -3 =$ _____

5 $-15 \times 15 =$ _____

6 $-12 \times -5 \times -5 =$ _____

7 $-2 \times 14 =$ _____

8 $-11 \times 21 =$ _____

9 $-15 \times -5 \times 3 =$ _____

10 $-3 \times -103 \times -2 =$ _____

11 $-20 \div -20 \times 14 =$ _____

12 $-22 \times 11 \times -10 =$ _____

13 $-8 \times -14 =$ _____

14 $-132 \div 44 =$ _____

15 $(150 \div -30) \times -3 =$ _____

16 $55 \div -55 \div -12 =$ _____

17 $(-25 \div (-3 \times 10)) \div -15 =$ _____

18 $52 \times -13 \div -4 =$ _____

Unit Test

Lessons 10–12

Restate in exponential form, then calculate.

1 $4 \times 4 \times 4 + 3 \times 3 \times 3$

_____

2 $3 \times 3 \times 2 \times 2 - 3 \times 3 \times 3$

_____

3 $4 \times 4 \times 4 \times 2 \times 2 + 4 \times 4 + 6 \times 6 - 3 \times 3$

_____

Restate using scientific notation.

4 13,224,714.066

_____

5 25,354.011

_____

6 .180705

_____

7 22,294,698,171.7

_____

8 866.0506

_____

9 118.6591

_____

Calculate using Order of Operations (PEMDAS).

10 $4 \times 2(8 - 4) + (12 - 6) \times 2 + (6 - 4) \times 3 + 22$

_____

11 $12 + 2(7 - 5) + (5 - 2) \times 2 + 2(6 - 2)$

_____

12 $22 + (2 \times 5) \times 2 + 2(7 - 3)$

_____

13 $36 - 3(6 - 2) + 7 \times 3 + 2(5) - 4$

_____

Lessons 10–12

Calculate.

14 4^3

_____

15 6^3

_____

16 $2^5 \times 2^{-3}$

_____

17 $10^9 \div 10^7$

_____

18 $12^{11} \times 12^{-11}$

_____

19 $\sqrt{64}$

_____

20 $\sqrt{144}$

_____

21 $\sqrt{625}$

_____

22 $\sqrt{196}$

_____

23 $\sqrt{2.25}$

_____

24 $\sqrt{1.69}$

_____

25 $\sqrt{8100}$

_____

Identify the number property that each expression displays.

26 $44(1) = 44$

_____

27 $19 + 0 = 19$

_____

28 $6 + (7 + 6) = (6 + 7) + 6$

_____

29 $3(7 + 3) = 3(7) + 3(3)$

_____

30 $14 + 16 + 20 = 20 + 16 + 14$

_____

31 $17 = 8 + 9, \quad 17 - 15 = 8 + 9 - 15$

_____

32 $43 \times 0 = 0$

_____

33 $35 = 18 + 17, \quad 35 + 9 = 18 + 17 + 9$

_____

Unit Test

Lessons 10–12

Solve the equation and indicate the point on the number line that corresponds with the answer.

```
        D B   A   C
  ←+--+--+--+--+--+--+--+--+--+--+--+--+--+--+--+--+--+--+--+--+--+→
   -10-9 -8 -7 -6 -5 -4 -3 -2 -1  0  1  2  3  4  5  6  7  8  9 10
```

34 $-5 + 5 - 5$

_____ 0 _____

35 $-10 + 4 - 1$

_____

36 $-7 + (-4) + 3$

_____

37 $9 - 5 + (-7)$

_____

Calculate.

38 -60×25

_____

39 $-135 \div 15$

_____

40 $12 \times (-5 - 7) \div (8 - 16)$

_____

41 $630 \div -70$

_____

42 $14(-6) \div -7$

_____

43 $-5 \times (-3) \times (14 - 18)$

_____

44 $-24 \times -3 \div -2$

_____

45 $15 \times -3 \div 9$

_____

46 $(19 - 23) \times (5 - 4) \times (17 - 15)$

_____

Understanding Variable Expressions

Sometimes you want to solve a problem to find an unknown number. The unknown number is called a **variable**. A variable is a letter that represents a number. A common variable used in algebra is x. But you will see any letter used as a variable (a, b, c, d, etc.). An **algebraic expression** is a letter, a number, or a combination of the two, connected by some mathematical operation such as addition, subtraction, multiplication, or division.

When you have a variable in a multiplication expression, you don't need to use the multiplication symbol. So $12 \times m$ is usually written as $12m$. The 12 is called a **coefficient**, which is a number that multiplies a variable.

Some algebraic expressions:

$$n + 19 \qquad (p - 72) \times 3 \qquad \frac{b}{3}$$
$$(36 \div g) + 9 \qquad 12 \times m$$

Sometimes you will need to translate algebraic expressions into words. Other times you will translate a phrase into an algebraic expression. This will help you understand the algebra exercise.

Examples:

$x + 9$	the sum of a number and nine
$7x$	the product of 7 and a number
Six less than four times a number	$4x - 6$
A number divided by five plus 10	$\frac{n}{5} + 10$

Remember...

A variable is a letter that represents a number. A common variable is x but can be any letter in the alphabet. The fact that a letter is used in a mathematical exercise should not confuse you. Since the letter represents a number, you treat it like a number when you complete exercises involving variables.

Exercises   EXPLAIN

Write in words what each expression is describing.

1 $\frac{a}{2} + 22$ _____

2 $y + 4$ _____

3 $4b + 3$ _____

4 $.9q - 9$ _____

5 $(x - 4) \div 20$ _____

6 $(3g + 7) - 8 + 33$ _____

7 $3n - 9$ _____

8 $\frac{5}{h}$ _____

13.2

Solving Equations with Addition and Subtraction

You learned the Equality Properties of Addition and Subtraction, which say that if you add or subtract a number from one side of an equation, you must add or subtract the same number from the other side of the equation. This rule is important when you are solving equations that use addition and subtraction.

Example:

Problem: $z - 32 = 51$. Find z.

Can you add 32 to the left side of the equation to leave z by itself? You can do that, but you also have to add 32 to the right side of the equation.

Step 1: Add the same number to both sides of the equation: $z = 51 + 32$

Step 2: Add: $51 + 32 = 83$
So $z = 83$

Example:

Problem: $d + 9 = 21$. Find d.

This time, you can subtract 9 from the left side of the equation to leave d by itself. But you have to subtract 9 from the right side of the equation, too.

Step 1: Subtract the same number from both sides of the equation: $d = 21 - 9$

Step 2: Subtract: $21 - 9 = 12$
So $d = 12$

Exercises   SOLVE

1 $x + 9 = 17$

2 $17 = s + 8$

3 $14 + z = 49$

4 $17 - f = 14$

5 $m - 30 = 35$

6 $c - 22 = 22$

7 $y + 11 = 42$

8 $107 = 17 + l$

9 $k + 28 = 64$

10 $28 + u = 43$

11 $59 - t = 42$

12 $13 - a = 4$

13 $24 + b = 54$

14 $54 - e = 22$

15 $15 + d = 39$

Solving Equations with Multiplication and Division

Division is the "opposite" of multiplication, and multiplication is the "opposite" of division. If you multiply an original number by a second number, and then divide the product by the second number, you are left with the original number.

For example: $3 \times 5 \div 5 = 3$

If you divide an original number by a second number, and then multiply the quotient by the second number, you will are left with the original number.

For example: $6 \div 3 \times 3 = 6$

If you have a fraction with the same number in the numerator and denominator, the fraction is equal to 1. So $\frac{5}{5} = 1$, $\frac{3}{3} = 1$, and $\frac{w}{w} = 1$. (You do not even need to know the value of w!)

Remember...

In an equation, you need to treat both sides in the same way. Whatever you do to one side, you must also do to the other side.

Examples:

$\frac{k}{5} = 12$. Solve for k.

Since $\frac{k}{5} = k \times \frac{1}{5}$, you multiply the left side of the equation by 5. Then you would have $k \times 1$, which is equal to k alone. You can multiply the left side by 5 *only* if you *also* multiply the right side by 5.

Step 1: Multiply both sides by the same number:
$k = 12 \times 5$

Step 2: Multiply: $12 \times 5 = 60$
So $k = 60$

$7u = 56$. Solve for u.

Now, you divide the left side by 7 to get u. Of course, you must *also* divide the right side by 7.

Step 1: $u = 56 \div 7$

Step 2: Divide: $56 \div 7 = 8$
So $u = 8$

Exercises SOLVE

1 $7n = 49$

2 $\frac{q}{5} = 9$

3 $12f = 84$

4 $\frac{42}{b} = 14$

5 $3k = 39$

6 $55 \div s = 11$

7 $\frac{m}{30} = 4$

8 $16h = 112$

9 $\frac{x}{15} = 6$

10 $4n = 56$

11 $18m = 72$

12 $11d = 143$

Name _____

Solving 2-Step Equations

Sometimes when solving an equation the process can take more than one step. When you cannot simply add or subtract a number or multiply the coefficient in front of the variable by its multiplicative inverse, you may need to take two steps to solve for the variable. After combining like terms you need to get the variable on one side (traditionally the left) and the number on the right. Once you have done this, you multiply both sides of the equation by the multiplicative inverse of the coefficient of the variable.

Example: $3x + 7 = 12$

Step 1: Subtract 7 from both sides: $3x = 12 - 7$

Step 2: Divide both sides by 3: $x = \frac{5}{3}$

So $x = \frac{5}{3}$

Exercises   SOLVE

1 $10x - 7 = 23$ _____

_____

2 $14 = 12 + 2x$ _____

_____

3 $21 + 4x = 28$ _____

_____

4 $200 + 15x = 425$ _____

_____

5 $5x + 39 = 41$ _____

_____

6 $10z + 17 = 77$ _____

_____

7 $65 = 41 + 3x$ _____

_____

8 $107 = 75 + 16r$ _____

_____

9 $49 + 18d = 37$ _____

_____

10 $15b + 18 = 30$ _____

_____

11 $5q = 10q + 60$ _____

_____

12 $2f + 4f + 18 = 32$ _____

_____

13 $3j = 5j - 14$ _____

_____

14 $23 + 18r = 6r + 47$ _____

_____

15 $13k + 14k + 10 = 13$ _____

_____

16 $14v = 10v - 5$ _____

_____

Plotting Ordered Pairs

All points on a grid can be expressed,
or identified, by using two numbers.

Example:

Find the first number by looking along the X-axis
(the horizontal line). Put your finger on that spot. If
you move your finger up and down in a vertical line,
you will still be at the same X number. To find the
exact point you want, look at the second number.
This second number tells you where to move your
finger along the vertical line. In the diagram, Point A
is written as (2,4). Point B is written as (3,1).

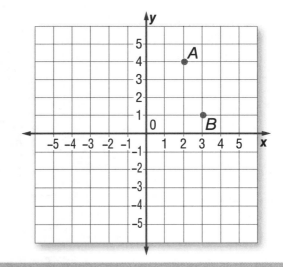

Exercises **GRAPH**

Graph #1

1. Plot the following
   ordered pairs on
   the graph:

   A (4,2)

   B (6,−6)

   C (−8,−8)

   D (−4,4)

   E (5,5)

   F (2,9)

   G (3,4)

   H (−4,−3)

   I (−5,−5)

   J (6,−1)

   K (−3,−3)

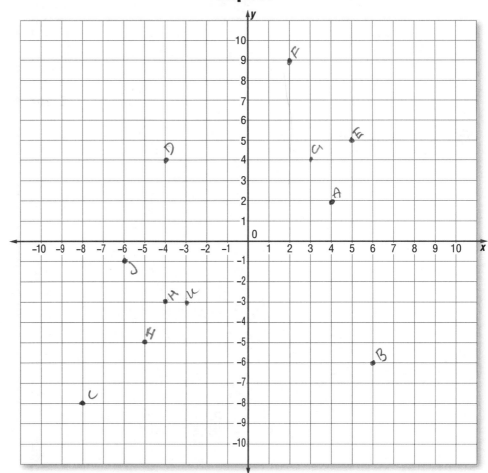

Name 3/28/2023

Graph #2

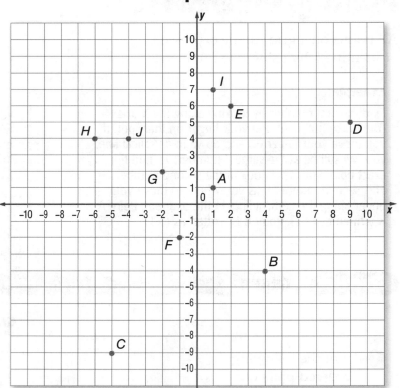

② Give the coordinates for each point on the graph:

A 1,1

B 4,-4

C -5,-9

D 9,5

E 2,6

F -1,-2

G -2,2

H -6,4

I 1,7

J -4,4

Graph #3

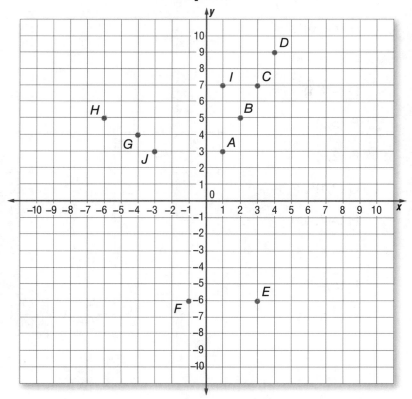

③ Give the coordinates for each point on the graph:

A 1,3

B 2,5

C 3,7

D 4,9

E 3,-6

F -1,-6

G -4,4

H -6,5

I 1,7

J -3,3

Function Tables

Can you make a graph of an equation? Yes, you can draw a function such as $y = 3x + 2$ on a graph, you just need a number of order pairs (x, y) to plot on the coordinate plane. The easiest way to do this is to make a **function table**.

To generate a function table, you substitute a number of values of x in the equation, and then complete the equation to determine the value of y. The function table allows you to make a

record of these ordered pairs so that you can quickly plot the points. When choosing values of x to substitute in the equation, it is good to use whole numbers that will likely generate whole-number values for y. These are easier to plot.

Using $x = 0$ is always a good value. Also, when the function has an exponent, make sure that you use some negative numbers.

Exercises   CALCULATE

Fill in the corresponding values of y for the given x value in the function table.

1 $y = x + 1$

x	y
0	1
1	2
2	3
3	4
4	5
5	6

2 $y = 2x + 2$

x	y
−2	−2
−1	0
0	2
1	4
2	6
3	8

3 $y = x - 4$

x	y
0	−4
1	−3
4	0
6	2
8	4
10	6

4 $y = 2x - 3$

x	y
−1	−5
0	−3
1	−1
2	1
3	3
5	7

⑤ $y = 2x + 1$

x	y
−2	−3
1	3
0	1
2	5
4	9
6	13

⑥ $y = \frac{1}{2}x + 1$

x	y
−4	−1
−2	0
0	1
2	2
4	3
6	4

Identify the function by looking at the ordered pairs (x, y) in the function table.

⑦ $x + 2 = y$

x	y
0	2
1	3
2	4
3	5
4	6
5	7

⑧ $2x + 9 = y$

x	y
−2	5
−1	7
0	9
2	13
4	17
5	19

⑨ $x^2 + 2 = y$

x	y
−4	18
−2	6
0	2
2	6
3	11
4	18

⑩ $x^3 = y$

x	y
−3	−27
−2	−8
0	0
1	1
2	8
3	27

Solve Equations by Graphing

One way to determine the point of intersection of two lines is to graph the lines and see where they meet. The process takes three steps:

1. Create function tables for each line.

2. Plot the two lines on a coordinate plane.

3. Visually assess the lines to determine the point of intersection.

This method will enable you to make a good estimation of the point of intersection of the lines. Sometimes the two lines will meet at a point where the ordered pair (x, y) has integer values for both x and y, but many times they will not. So, you will have to make an estimation of the coordinates of the point of intersection.

Exercises   GRAPH

Determine the point of intersection of the two lines.

① $y = x + 3$

x	y

$y = 2x + 1$

x	y

2 $y = x - 4$

x	y

$y = -x + 2$

x	y

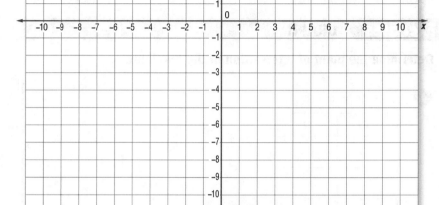

3 $y = 4x - 3$

x	y

$y = x$

x	y

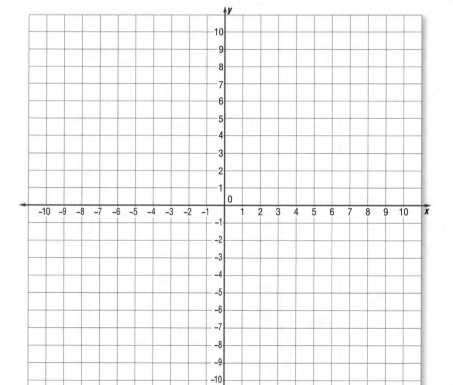

Lessons 13–14

Describe in words the following expressions.

1 $2x + 15$

_____

2 $5y - 12$

_____

Solve for x.

3 $x + 4 = 7$ **4** $x + 8 = 124$ **5** $x + 2 = 7$ **6** $x + 9 = 14$

_____   _____   _____   _____

7 $x - 6 = 4$ **8** $x - 11 = 5$ **9** $x - 2 = 13$ **10** $x - 5 = 9$

_____   _____   _____   _____

Solve for y.

11 $3y - 5 = 7$ **12** $2y + 3 = 11$ **13** $4y - 3 = 13$ **14** $2y - 7 = 9$

_____   _____   _____   _____

15 $6y - 6 = 18$ **16** $7y - 14 = 28$ **17** $16y + 24 = 56$ **18** $12y - 24 = 48$

_____   _____   _____   _____

Unit Test

Lessons 13–14

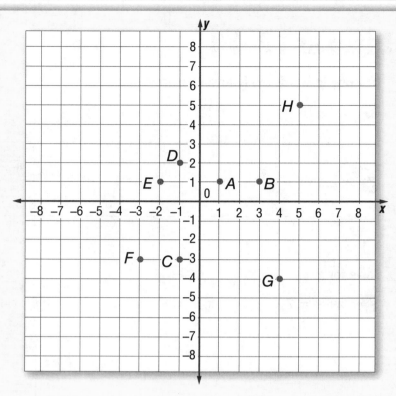

Give the coordinates for each point.

19 A _____ **20** B _____ **21** C _____ **22** D _____

23 E _____ **24** F _____ **25** G _____ **26** H _____

Plot the following points on the grid.

27 Point A (6,6)

Point B (−3,−3)

Point C (−1,2)

Point D (3,−2)

Point E (4,−2)

Point F (−4,2)

Point G (−6,−6)

Point H (−1,3)

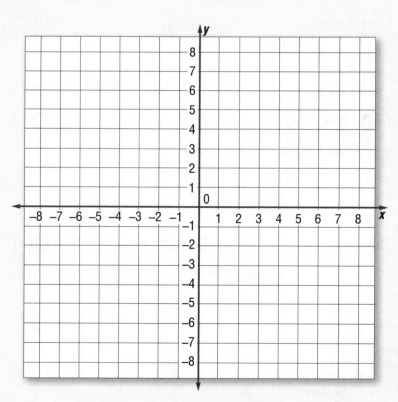

Lessons 13–14

Create a function table for $2x + 1$ and plot the ordered pairs on the grid.

28

$2x + 1$

x	y

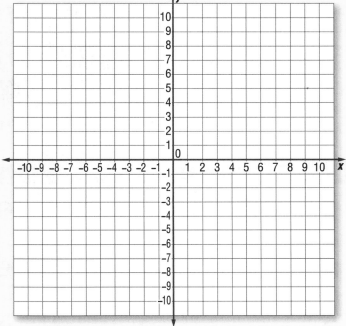

Create function tables for $2x - 1$ and $x + 3$. Plot the ordered pairs and determine the value of x where the equation $2x - 1 = x + 3$ is true.

29

$2x - 1$

x	y

$x + 3$

x	y

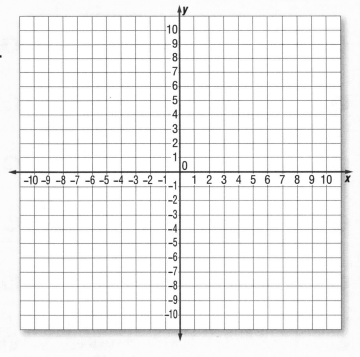

Customary Units of Length

The **customary units of length** are inches (in.), feet (ft), yards (yd), and miles (mi). You can compare them to each other, and even convert one to another by using simple calculations.

1 foot = 12 in.

1 yard = 3 ft

1 mile = 1,760 yd or 5,280 ft

Remember...

You do *not* need to add the plural *s* when you abbreviate units of measure.

Exercises CONVERT

1 72 in. = _____ ft

2 12 ft = _____ in.

3 3 ft 8 in. = _____ in.

4 192 in. = _____ ft

5 7,920 ft = _____ mi

6 16 ft 6 in. = _____ yd

7 4 ft 9 in. = _____ in.

8 1056 ft = _____ mi

9 $\frac{4}{5}$ mi = _____ in.

10 66 in. = _____ ft

11 648 in. = _____ yd

12 $7\frac{1}{2}$ yd = _____ ft = _____ in.

13 35 ft = _____ yd

14 16 yd 2 ft = _____ in.

15 2 mi 303 yd = _____ ft

16 34 yd 2 ft = _____ in.

17 The river is 768 yards wide where the city plans to build a new bridge. How many 32-foot sections of bridge will the city engineers need in order to build the bridge?

_____

18 Patty wants to know how far she can throw a softball. After throwing, she estimates that the ball traveled 1,764 inches.

How many yards is that? _____

How many feet? _____

Customary Units of Liquid Volume

When you buy a bottle of juice, or when you add a liquid to a recipe, you will often measure in units of **liquid volume**. Liquid volume is the amount of liquid a container can hold. Liquid volume is measured in cups (c), pints (pt), quarts (qt), and gallons (gal). Just like units of length, you can compare these units to each other, and change one to another by using simple calculations.

1 pint = 2 cups   1 quart = 2 pints
1 gallon = 4 quarts

Example:

How many cups are in a gallon?

Step 1: You know that there are 4 quarts in a gallon, and there are 2 pints in a quart. So multiply the number of quarts × 2 to find out how many pints are in a gallon.

Step 2: 4 × 2 = 8 pints in a gallon.

Step 3: You know that there are 2 cups in a pint. So multiply the number of pints × 2.

Step 4: 8 × 2 = 16 cups in a gallon.

Exercises   CONVERT

1 72 c = _____ qt

2 12 qt = _____ c

3 3 qt 1 pt = _____ c

4 192 gal = _____ qt

5 328 qt = _____ gal

6 2 gal 1 qt = _____ c

7 6 qt 1 c = _____ c

8 52 c = _____ qt

9 $\frac{3}{4}$ gal = _____ c

10 66 pt = _____ gal

11 4 qt 1 c = _____ c

12 $7\frac{1}{2}$ qt = _____ gal = _____ c

13 35 qt 3 c = _____ gal

14 256 c = _____ gal

15 132 c = _____ pt = _____ qt

16 34 gal 1 qt = _____ pt

17 Allison's aquarium holds 25 gallons of water. One quart of water evaporated from the aquarium. How much water is left in the aquarium?

_____

18 Bobby drinks 1 quart and 1 cup of water for every 3 miles he runs. If he runs 9 miles, how much water should he drink?

_____

15.3

Customary Units of Weight

Can you name the **customary units of weight**? Weight is customarily measured in ounces (oz), pounds (lb), and tons (T). As with units of length and liquid volume, you can compare units of weight to each other, and change one to another by using simple calculations.

1 pound = 16 oz

1 ton = 2,000 lb

Example:

How many ounces are in three pounds?

Step 1: You know that there are 16 oz in one pound. So multiply the number of ounces in one pound by three.

Step 2: $16 \times 3 = 48$ ounces in three pounds.

Exercises   CONVERT

1. 86 oz = _____ lb

2. 8 lb 5 oz = _____ oz

3. 10 T = _____ lb

4. 2400 lb = _____ T

5. 166 oz = _____ lb

6. 13 lb 6 oz = _____ oz

7. $\frac{1}{4}$ T = _____ lb

8. $\frac{2}{5}$ T = _____ lb

9. 2 lb 12 oz + 2 lb 5 oz = _____ oz

10. 104 oz = _____ lb

11. Barton's backpack weighs 498 ounces. How many pounds does the backpack weigh?

    _____

12. If Jason weighed 167 lb and he lost 112 oz during the summer, how much does he weigh after losing the weight?

    _____

13. Kathleen weighed her two cats. The first cat weighed 7 lb 12 oz and the second weighed 11 lb 15 oz. How much did the two cats weigh in total?

    _____

14. Freddie's camping gear weighs 70 lb in total. He adds an extra pair of shoes which weighs 2 lb 4 oz and removes tent stakes that weigh 6 lb 8 oz. How much does the gear weigh now?

    _____

Perimeter with Customary Units

Imagine that you want to find the length around a figure. How can you measure that? You want to find the figure's **perimeter**, or the distance around it. To find the perimeter of a figure, add the lengths of all of its sides.

Examples:

The perimeter of this triangle is $3 + 4 + 5 = 12$ in.

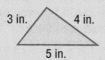

You could change this total number into feet by dividing the number of inches by 12.

$\frac{12}{12} = 1$ ft

The perimeter of this rectangle is
$8 + 4 + 8 + 4 = 24$ ft

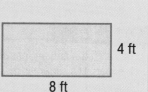

You could change this total into inches by multiplying by 12.

$24 \times 12 = 288$ feet

Exercises CALCULATE

1 What is the perimeter of the figure shown?

_____

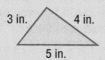

2 What is the perimeter of the figure shown?

_____

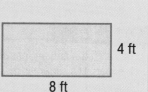

3 What is the perimeter of the triangle?

_____

4 What is the perimeter of the figure shown?

_____

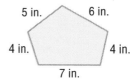

5 What is the perimeter of the figure shown?

_____

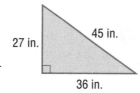

6 What is the perimeter of the figure shown?

_____

7 Jane created the odd-shaped wheel pictured in the figure. If she were to push the wheel 3 times around, how far would she have pushed the wheel?

_____

Area with Customary Units

Sometimes, you want to know a figure's **area**, or the number of units it would take to fill it. Those units are called square inches, square feet, square yards, or even square miles.

Remember...

Be careful! A square foot *does not equal* 12 square inches. It equals 144 square inches. A square yard *does not equal* 3 square feet. It equals 9 square feet.

Examples:

The area of a *rectangle* is its length (*l*) × its width (*w*).

8 in. × 4 in. = 32 square in.

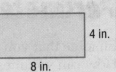

A *square* is a special kind of rectangle, with all of its sides equal in length. You may remember that a number to the second power, or a number multiplied once by itself, is called "squared."

4 yd × 4 yd = 16 square yards

The area of a *triangle* is $\frac{1}{2}$ × base (*b*) × height (*h*).

$\frac{1}{2}$ × 3 ft × 4 ft = 6 sq ft

Exercises   CALCULATE

1 What is the area of the rectangle?

_____

6 in.   5 in.

2 What is the area of the square?

_____

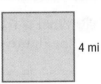
4 mi   4 mi

3 What is the area of the triangle?

_____

4 in.   5 in.   3 in.

4 What is the area of the square?

_____

6 in.

5 What is the area of the rectangle?

_____

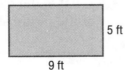
9 ft   5 ft

6 What is the area of the triangle?

_____

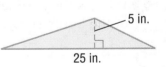
5 in.   25 in.

7 What is the area of the square?

_____

3 in.

8 What is the area of the rectangle?

_____

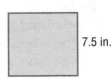
8 in.   7.5 in.

Metric Units of Length

You may have heard of metric units. These units are much easier to work with mathematically than customary units. That is because metric units are all based on the **powers of 10**. The **metric units of length** are millimeters (mm), centimeters (cm), meters (m), and kilometers (km).

$$1 \text{ centimeter} = 10 \text{ mm}$$
$$1 \text{ meter} = 100 \text{ cm}$$
$$1 \text{ kilometer} = 1000 \text{ m}$$

Remember...

To make calculations simpler for yourself, learn these prefixes:

milli = thousandth   centi = hundredth   kilo = thousand

Example:

How many cm = 35 m?

  Step 1: Think: 100 cm = 1 m

  Step 2: Multiply the number of meters × 100.

You can do this by regular multiplication.

$$35 \times 100 = 3500$$

However, it is much easier to move the decimal point two places to the right.

35 m = 3500 cm

How many m = 465 mm?

  Step 1: Think: 1000 mm = 1 m

  Step 2: Divide: $465 \div 1000 = \dfrac{465}{1000}$

You can also do this calculation by moving the decimal point three places to the left.

456 mm = .456 m

Exercises   CONVERT

1 210 m = _____ km

2 145 mm = _____ cm

3 573 m = _____ cm

4 26 m = _____ mm

5 400 cm = _____ km

6 400 m = _____ cm

7 1.6 m = _____ mm

8 2.5 km = _____ m

9 116 mm = _____ m

10 1.557 km = _____ mm

11 4355 mm = _____ cm

12 .4667 km = _____ cm

13 3.0556 m = _____ mm

14 Terry covered the outside edge of his cousin's monster truck tires with a border of fluorescent yellow paint. If each tire measured 6.25 meters around the outside edge, then how many centimeters of edging did he paint on one tire?

_____

15 The distance from Mike's house to the school is .775 kilometers. How many meters is that?

_____

16.2

Metric Units of Liquid Volume

The basic **metric unit of liquid volume** is the **liter** (L). There are also milliliters (mL) and kiloliters (kL).

You can probably figure that:

1 liter = 1,000 mL   1 kiloliter = 1,000 L

Remember...
All metric units are powers of 10.

Example:
How many milliliters are in 3.5 liters?
Step 1: Think: 1000 mL = 1 liter
Step 2: Multiply 1000 by 3.5 = 3500 mL

Exercises CONVERT

1 873 mL = _____ L

2 1455 mL = _____ kL

3 4.75 L = _____ mL

4 7945 mL = _____ L

5 100 mL = _____ kL

6 2554 mL = _____ L

7 .0025 L = _____ mL

8 .007 kL = _____ mL

9 Pam's recipe calls for 3.4 L of olive oil. Unfortunately, all she has is a measuring cup that holds 10 mL. How many times will she have to fill her measuring cup with olive oil to complete the recipe?

_____

10 Ron mixed 4,500 milliliters of his favorite paint color. How many 1-liter containers can he fill with the mixture?

_____

11 Harriet had 5.768 liters of special-liquid cleanser before she gave 554 mL of it to her mother, and 1.4 mL to her younger sister. How much liquid cleanser does she have left?

_____

12 The science teacher instructs the students to add 256 mL of Liquid A to 1.5 L of Liquid B. How much liquid will there be altogether, assuming nothing evaporates or turns to a solid?

_____

Metric Units of Mass

The basic **metric unit of mass** is the **gram** (g). There are also milligrams (mg), centigrams (cg), and kilograms (kg).

Since you know about metric prefixes, you could probably make the following list yourself!

1 cg = 10 mg   1 g = 100 cg   1 kg = 1,000 g

Examples:
How many grams are in an object that has a mass of 4.25 kilograms?

Step 1: Think: 1000 grams = 1 kilogram

Step 2: Multiply: 4.25 × 1000 = 4250 grams

Exercises CONVERT

1. 400 g = _____ kg

2. 225 kg = _____ mg

3. 6600 g = _____ kg

4. 4505 mg = _____ g

5. 21.35 kg = _____ mg

6. 530 mg = _____ g

7. 650 mg = _____ g

8. 71 kg = _____ cg

9. 3.721 kg = _____ g

10. 2313 g = _____ kg

11. 546 mg = _____ g

12. 12,305 g = _____ kg

13. 4430 mg = _____ g

14. 12.34 kg = _____ g

15. 2 mg = _____ kg

16. 300 kg = _____ mg

17. 258 mg = _____ cg

18. 65 g = _____ kg

19. Larry has 5,599.4 milligrams of saffron seasoning that he brought back from India. He sells 1.06 grams to a local health food restaurant, and he gives his mother .0034 kg. How much saffron does Larry have left?

_____

20. Richard keeps three bee hives in his backyard. He collected 1,678.616 grams of honey from the first hive, 1.6 kilograms from the second hive, and 1,660,301 milligrams from the third hive. Which hive produced the most honey?

_____

How much more honey did it produce than the hive that produced the second most amount of honey?

_____

Calculating Perimeter and Area with Metric Units

You can also use metric units to calculate perimeter and area. You perform exactly the same kinds of calculations as when you are working with customary units of length. The only difference is that when you work with metric units, your answers will be expressed in metric units.

Perimeter is expressed in mm, cm, m, or km.

Area is expressed in sq mm, sq cm, sq m, or sq km.

Remember...

Do not change between metric units.
For example, 1 sq km does not = 1,000 sq m

Exercises   CALCULATE

1 What is the perimeter of a square with sides of 10 cm?

10 cm
10 cm

_____

What is the area?

_____

2 What is the perimeter of the figure?

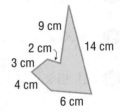

9 cm
2 cm
3 cm
4 cm
14 cm
6 cm

_____

3 A rectangle has sides of 4.4 cm and 6 cm. What is the perimeter of the rectangle?

_____

What is the area?

_____

4 What is the perimeter of a rectangle with 2 sides of 12 meters and 2 sides of 6 meters?

_____

What is the area?

_____

5 What is the area of the triangle?

_____

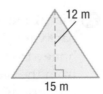

12 m
15 m

6 What is the area of the triangle?

_____

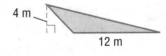

4 m
12 m

7 Ariel is cleaning a rug that is 4.2 meters long and 3 meters wide. If the dry cleaning store charges $18.00 per square meter to clean it, how much will she pay to clean the rug? _____

What is the perimeter of the rug? _____

Changing from Customary Units to Metric Units

Can you change customary units to metric units? Yes. Here is a chart to guide you. Keep in mind that some of the metric units are not exact, but they are pretty close.

There is one customary unit on the chart that you may not recognize. In some parts of the world, beverages are often measured in **fluid ounces**.

Length	Liquid Volume	Weight or Mass
1 inch = 2.54 centimeters	1 cup = .237 liters	1 ounce = 28.35 grams
1 foot = .305 meters	1 pint = .473 liters	1 pound = .454 kilograms
1 yard = .914 meters	1 quart = .946 liters	1 ton = 907.18 kilograms
1 mile = 1.609 kilometers	1 gallon = 3.785 liters	
	1 fluid ounce = 29.574 milliliters	

Exercises CONVERT

1 14 in. = _____ cm

2 15 ft = _____ m

3 12 yd = _____ m

4 4 yd = _____ m

5 3 mi = _____ km

6 4 c = _____ L

7 3 pt = _____ L

8 9 qt = _____ L

9 3.5 gal = _____ L

10 11 fl oz = _____ mL

11 14 oz = _____ g

12 3 lbs = _____ kg

13 6 oz = _____ g

14 2 mi = _____ m

15 11 c = _____ L

16 Which would be heavier: 4.8 lb or 2000 g of silver? _____

17 About how many meters tall is a 120-ft building?

_____

18 Farah's cooler holds 8 qt of liquid. About how many mL will it hold?

_____

Name _____

Changing from Metric Units to Customary Units

Since customary units can be changed to metric units, you can also reverse this process. Again, remember that some of the numbers on the chart below are not exact. However, they are all close.

Length	Liquid Volume	Weight or Mass
1 millimeter = .039 inches	1 liter = 1.057 quarts	1 gram = .035 ounces
1 centimeter = .394 inches	1 kiloliter = 264.2 gallons	1 kilogram = 2.205 pounds
1 meter = 39.37 inches		
1 kilometer = .621 miles		

Exercises **CONVERT**

1 24 mm = _____ in.

2 143 cm = _____ in.

3 3 m = _____ in.

4 4 km = _____ mi

5 20 g = _____ oz

6 6 L = _____ qt

7 3 kL = _____ gal

8 4.5 kg = _____ lb

9 242 mm = _____ in.

10 13 kg is about how many oz? _____

11 1100 mm = _____ in.

12 2 kg + 32 g = _____ oz

13 The average player on the school basketball team is 190 centimeters tall. The average volleyball player is 6 ft 4 inches tall. Which team has a taller average height?

_____

14 The Booster Club sponsored a 10-km walk to raise money for charity. About how many miles is the length of the walk?

_____

Customary and Metric Units of Temperature

The units used to describe temperature are called **degrees**. Degrees are written with a small circle at the top right of a number: 30 degrees = 30°. Customary degrees are measured on the **Fahrenheit** scale. You must add the word Fahrenheit (or just F), because other temperature scales that are *not* customary are also used to describe temperature.

The metric unit to describe temperature is called the **Celsius** degree (or just C). This is also sometimes referred to as **Centigrade**.

The Celsius scale is used in scientific work and is easier to use than the Fahrenheit scale. Even though both are expressed in degrees, a Celsius degree *does not* equal a Fahrenheit degree!

You can change Celsius to Fahrenheit temperatures, or Fahrenheit to Celsius temperatures. To do so, you must use the following equations:

$$(F - 32) \times \left(\frac{5}{9}\right) = C \qquad C \times \left(\frac{9}{5}\right) + 32 = F$$

Celsius	Fahrenheit	
0° C	32° F	Freezing point of water
100° C	212° F	Boiling point of water
35° C	95° F	Hot air temperature
37° C	98.6° F	Human body temperature

Example:

Convert 98.6° F to C.

Step 1: Set up the equation:
$$(98.6 - 32) \times \left(\frac{5}{9}\right) = C$$

Step 2: Calculate: $66.6 \times \frac{5}{9} = 37$
$$98.6° F = 37° C$$

Exercises CONVERT

1 150° C = _____ F

2 150° F = _____ C

3 0° C = _____ F

4 0° F = _____ C

5 216° F = _____ C

6 105° C = _____ F

7 72° F = _____ C

8 30° C = _____ F

9 −25° F = _____ C

10 35° F = _____ C

11 37° C = _____ F

12 950° C = _____ F

13 The melting point of aluminum is 1,219° F and the melting point of nickel is 2,646° F. What is the temperature difference between the two melting points? Express your answer in degrees Celsius.

_____

14 Jamie took his temperature with a Celsius thermometer, and it read 38° C. What would his temperature be in degrees Fahrenheit?

_____

Unit Test

Lessons 15–17

1 Manny is going to replace the trim around the windows in his house. The trim for each window measures $10\frac{1}{2}$ feet. If Manny has 15 windows in his house, how many inches of trim does he need to replace?

_____

2 Annie's fish tank holds $39\frac{1}{2}$ gallons of water. She is using a 1 quart container to fill the tank. How many full containers will Annie need to fill the tank?

_____

3 Florence weighed boxes for the shipping department. The first box weighed 196 ounces. The second box weighed $13\frac{3}{8}$ pounds. Which box weighed more?

_____

4 Mandie plans to paint the side of her barn. The side measures 10 meters long and 5.5 meters high. How much area does Mandie need to cover with paint?

_____ square meters

5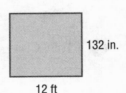

132 in.

12 ft

What is the area of the rectangle?

_____

What is the perimeter of the rectangle?

_____

6

12 ft   180 in.

9 ft

What is the area of the right triangle?

_____ square feet

What is the perimeter?

_____ inches

7 What is the area of the base of the rectangular box?

_____ square feet

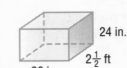

24 in.

$2\frac{1}{2}$ ft

36 in.

Lessons 15–17

8 A spacecraft must travel 24.1 kilometers per second to leave the Earth's atmosphere. How far does the spacecraft travel in a minute?

_____

In an hour? _____   In a day? _____

9 A school banner is 5.5 meters in length and 1,850 millimeters in width. How much fabric was used to make the banner?

_____ sq cm

10 Blanche has three cans of paint to mix. One can holds 1,957 milliliters of paint, the second can holds 115.6 centiliters of paint, and the third can holds 3.9 liters of paint. How much paint will Blanche mix?

_____ liters

11 What is the area of a triangle with sides of 12 cm, a base of 6 cm, and a height of 8 cm?

_____ sq cm

What is the perimeter of the triangle?

_____

8 cm
12 cm
6 cm

12 Frank walked around the entire rectangular school playground, which measures 126 meters by 6,500 centimeters. How far did Frank walk?

_____ meters

What is the area of the school playground?

_____ square meters

13 What is the area of a rectangle that measures 4.6 meters in width, and 5.5 meters in length?

_____ square meters

14 The average player on the soccer team weighs 165 pounds. About how much is that in kilograms?

_____

Unit Test

Name _____

Lessons 15–17

15 The average pickup truck has a gas tank that holds 95 liters of gasoline. How much is that in quarts and in gallons?

_____ quarts   _____ gallons

16 Pauline was looking for lawn-mowing jobs for the summer. She surveyed the neighborhood and found out that the average lawn measured 60 feet by 45 feet. What is the area in square feet?

_____ sq ft

About how much is the total area in square meters?

_____ sq meters

17 The distance of a flight from Cleveland to New Orleans is about 1,250 miles. The average speed of a commercial airliner is about 830 kilometers per hour. About how long will it take to fly from Cleveland to New Orleans?

_____ hours

18 The air conditioning company suggests that people keep the temperature in their homes between 22 and 28 degrees Celsius during the summer. What is the temperature range in degrees Fahrenheit?

_____

19

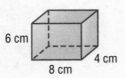

What is the area of the base of the rectangular solid shown?

_____

20

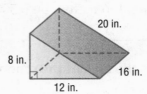

What is the area of the triangular face on the figure shown?

_____

21 In track and field, the standard middle distance event is the 5,000 meter race. About how many feet is 5,000 meters?

_____ feet

22 A body temperature of 103.6° F is considered an extremely high fever. What temperature is that in Celsius?

_____

Points and Lines

You probably used the words "point" and "line" before, but do those terms have special meaning in mathematics?

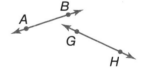

Yes, they do. You may think of a point as a dot, which is what we mean when we use "point" in everyday use. However, a **point** in mathematics is a specific location in space. It has no dimensions. A point is usually labeled with a capital letter.

A **line** is a straight path of points. A line goes in both directions and never ends. When we draw a line, we use a pencil so we can see it. A line drawn with a pencil has width and length.

However, a line in mathematics has only one dimension, length.

Because a line is a path of points, it can be named by *any* two points located *anywhere* on it, and you can use those points in either order. So in our illustration, Line $\overleftrightarrow{YZ}$ = Line $\overleftrightarrow{ZY}$, and Line $\overleftrightarrow{WX}$ = Line $\overleftrightarrow{XW}$.

Intersecting lines cross each other at a specific point. In this example, Lines $\overleftrightarrow{YZ}$ and $\overleftrightarrow{WX}$ cross at Point U.

Remember...

A line extends in *both* directions. It does not end in *either* direction.

Exercises   SOLVE

1 Draw the line denoted by $\overleftrightarrow{CD}$.

2 Draw $\overleftrightarrow{QR}$.

3 What would the single letter D indicate?

_____

4 What two lines are shown in the figure?

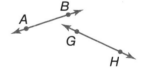

_____

_____

5 Describe in words what $\overleftrightarrow{JK}$ denotes.

_____

_____

_____

_____

6 Which of the following is *not* a line? _____

a. 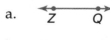 Z   Q

b. M N

c.

Line Segments and Rays

If lines go on forever in both directions, can you describe a line that ends at one or both sides? Yes, and there are some mathematical terms used to describe these.

A **line segment** is a specific part of a line that has ends at two points. It is named by its two end points. So Segment $\overline{ST}$ = Segment $\overline{TS}$. We can write it this way:

$$\overline{ST} = \overline{TS}$$

A **ray** is a part of a line that begins at a specific point, called a **vertex**, or **endpoint**. The line extends from that point in one direction without ending. To define a ray, you must use another letter along the line's path. Remember that the second letter is *not* the line's end. The *first* point in naming a ray is its vertex. So ray $\overrightarrow{QR}$ *does not* equal ray $\overleftarrow{RQ}$. Ray $\overrightarrow{QR}$ has a different vertex from ray $\overleftarrow{QR}$, and goes in the opposite direction.

Exercises SOLVE

1 Draw a diagram that illustrates a ray $\overrightarrow{YX}$.

2 Identify two rays and two line segments in the figure.

_____

_____

_____

_____

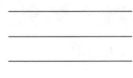

3 Identify three line segments in the diagram.

_____

_____

_____

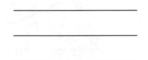

4 Draw two rays $\overrightarrow{AB}$ and $\overrightarrow{AC}$.

5 Identify the two line segments.

_____

_____

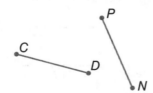

Measuring and Naming Angles

Do you think that rays from two intersecting lines can meet at the same point, or vertex? Yes they can. When they do, they form an **angle**, which is named by both its lines. The vertex is the middle letter of the angle's name.

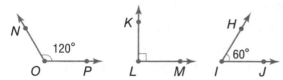

$\overrightarrow{NO}$ and $\overrightarrow{OP}$ intersect at point O, the vertex of each line, to form ∠NOP.

You measure angles in degrees. A straight line is 180°, so angles are always smaller than 180°. If an angle is greater than 90°, it is an **obtuse angle**. If it is less than 90°, it is an **acute angle**. If it is *exactly* 90°, it is a **right angle**. Right angles are often shown with a small square inside the angle.

∠NOP is an obtuse angle. ∠HIJ is an acute angle. ∠KLM is a right angle.

Exercises   IDENTIFY

Identify the angle as acute, right, or obtuse.

1 _____

2 _____

3 _____

4 _____

5 _____

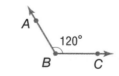

6 _____

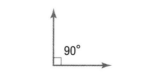

7 _____

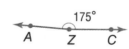

8 _____

Name _____

Types of Angles: Supplementary, Complementary, Interior, and Exterior

If angles always measure fewer degrees than a straight line, can two angles be added together to form 180°, or a straight line?

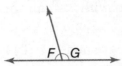

Yes, two angles that form a line are called **supplementary angles**. Their sum will equal 180°. So if you know the measurement of one angle, you can figure out the measure of the other angle. Notice that a single letter placed near the vertex can sometimes be used to identify angles.

If ∠F = 75°, you subtract this value from 180°. 180 − 75 equals angle G. Angle G = 105°.

Angles can have other kinds of relationships with each other. Two acute angles that form a right angle are called **complementary angles**. The sum of these two angles equals 90°.

So if ∠E = 35°, you subtract 35 from 90 to find angle D. Angle D = 55°.

Two intersecting lines always form four angles. The angles opposite each other are called **vertical angles**, and they are equal. ∠A = ∠C.   ∠B = ∠D.

Two different types of angles are created when a line intersects two parallel lines. Look at the figure below. Lines x and y are parallel and a line, or transversal, intersects, or crosses them. Eight angles are created and are labeled 1 through 8.

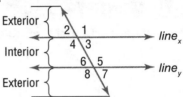

Angles 1, 2 ,7, and 8 are **exterior** angles because they are located outside parallel lines x and y.

Angles 3, 4, 5, and 6 are **interior** angles because they are between parallel lines x and y.

Remember...

You can prove that vertical angles are equal. In the example at the top of this column, angle A and angle B form a straight line. So angle A = 180° − angle B. Angle C and angle D also form a straight line. Angle C = 180°. So angle A = angle B.

Exercises IDENTIFY

1 From the figure below, give examples of two complementary, two supplementary and two vertical angles.

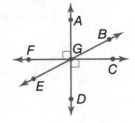

Complementary _____

Supplementary _____

Vertical _____

2 For the figure below, list all complementary and supplementary angles.

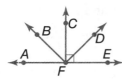

Complementary _____

_____

Supplementary _____

3

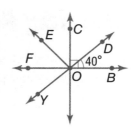

Are angle DOB and angle DOC complementary? _____

Explain. _____

_____

_____

4 In the figure below, a line is intersecting two parallel lines. Fill in the missing information:

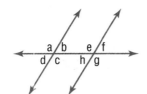

∠a = ∠_____ = ∠_____ = ∠_____

5 In the figure below, a line is intersecting two parallel lines. Fill in the missing angle measurements:

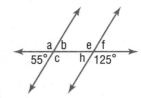

∠a = _____;   ∠b = _____;   ∠c = _____

∠e = _____;   ∠f = _____;   ∠h = _____

Name _____

Finding Missing Angle Measurements

Remember, when two parallel lines are intersected by another line, or transversal, eight angles are formed.

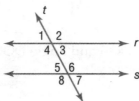

- Adjacent interior angles 4 and 5 and 3 and 6 are supplementary.
- Alternate interior angles 4 and 6 and 3 and 5 are equal.
- Adjacent exterior angles 1 and 8 and 2 and 7 are supplementary.
- Alternate exterior angles 1 and 7 and 2 and 8 are equal.

Exercises   SOLVE

1 Fill in the angle measurements for the other seven angles.

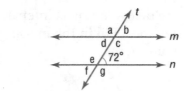

∠a _____   ∠b _____

∠c _____   ∠d _____

∠e _____   ∠f _____

∠g _____

2 Angle 3 is 48 degrees. List the measurements of the other seven angles.

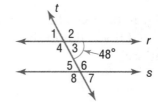

∠1 _____   ∠2 _____

∠4 _____   ∠5 _____

∠6 _____   ∠7 _____

∠8 _____

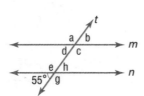

3 Fill in the angle measurements for the other seven angles.

∠a _____   ∠b _____

∠c _____   ∠d _____

∠e _____   ∠g _____

∠h _____

4 What is the measurement of ∠FOE? _____

What is the measurement of ∠EOC? _____

What is the measurement of ∠BOC? _____

Triangles: Acute, Right, Obtuse, Equilateral, Isosceles, and Scalene

A 2-dimensional figure with three sides is called a **triangle**. The three angles in a triangle always add up to 180°.

acute triangle   right triangle   obtuse triangle

All triangles have at least two angles that are acute. In an **acute triangle**, *all* three angles are acute. In a **right triangle**, one of the angles is a right angle. In an **obtuse triangle**, one of the angles is obtuse. Because *all three of its angles add up to 180°*, a triangle can have only one angle that measures 90° or more.

equilateral triangle   isosceles triangle   scalene triangle

Another way of looking at triangles is to look at the length of their sides. In an **equilateral triangle**, the three sides are the same length. They are **congruent**, or equal. In an **isosceles triangle**, two sides are congruent, but the third side is not. In a **scalene triangle**, none of the sides is congruent.

Exercises   IDENTIFY

Identify as acute, right, or obtuse.

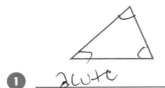

① _____acute_____

② _____obtuse_____

③ _____right_____

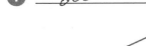

④ _____obtuge_____

⑤ _____right_____

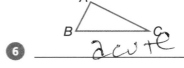

⑥ _____acute_____

Identify as isosceles, scalene, or equilateral.

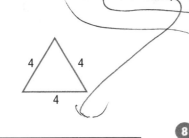 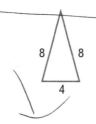 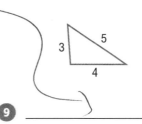

⑦ _____   ⑧ _____   ⑨ _____

Name _____

Triangles: Congruent and Similar

Similar triangles are triangles with the same shape, but with different sizes. Triangles that have the same angles are similar. The best example of this is an equilateral triangle, a triangle whose sides are all of equal length. Equilateral triangles have three equal angles of 60°. However, the sides of equilateral triangles can be different lengths. This is true of all triangles that have equal angles. The triangles look the same, but they can be different sizes.

Congruent triangles have equal sides and equal angles. They are the same, or **congruent**. Obviously, if two triangles are congruent they are also similar.

Exercises IDENTIFY

Identify each set of triangles as similar, congruent, or neither. Explain your answer.

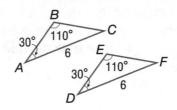

1 _____
_____
_____

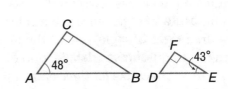

2 _____
_____
_____

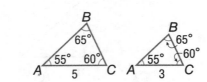

3 _____
_____
_____

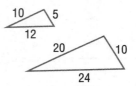

4 _____
_____
_____

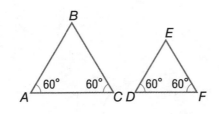

5 _____
_____
_____

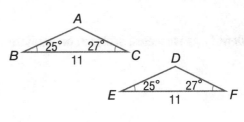

6 _____
_____
_____

Right Triangles and Pythagorean Theorem

The **Pythagorean Theorem** was developed a long time ago by a Greek mathematician after observing the special characteristics of right triangles. The theorem states that for all right triangles, the square of the length of the hypotenuse (the side opposite the right angle) is equal to the sum of the squares of lengths of the other two sides, or legs as they are also known.

In the figure, side c is the hypotenuse and sides a and b are the legs. So the Pythagorean Theorem states that the square of the hypotenuse equals the sum of the squares of the lengths of the other two sides, or $c^2 = a^2 + b^2$, where c is the hypotenuse and a and b are the legs.

Example: In the right triangle above, suppose the length of $a = 3$ and $b = 4$. What would the length of c equal?

Step 1: Set up the equation using the Pythagorean Theorem: $3^2 + 4^2 = c^2$

Step 2: Calculate: $9 + 16 = c^2$
$\sqrt{25} = c$
$c = 5$

Remember...

There are several special cases of right triangle that will help you to solve equations in the future. Look at the chart below for examples.

Side a	Side b	Hypotenuse
1	1	$\sqrt{2}$
3	4	5
6	8	10
5	12	13
9	12	15

Exercises   SOLVE

Use The Pythagorean Theorem to determine the length of the missing side.

1 If side A is 6 and side B is 8, then side C (the hypotenuse) is _____

2 If side A is 9 and side B is 9, then side C (the hypotenuse) is _____

3 If side A is 10 and side B is 24, then side C (the hypotenuse) is _____

4 If side A is 9 and side C (the hypotenuse) is 15, then side B is _____

5 If side B is 6 and the hypotenuse is 10, then side A is _____

6 If side A is 12 and side B is 5, then side C (the hypotenuse) is _____

Name _____

Right Triangles and Pythagorean Theorem (cont.)

You can also use the Pythagorean Theorem and the ratio of *similar* triangles to find the unknown lengths of sides.

Example: ABC and DEF are similar. That means the ratios of the sides are equal. You can use the ratios and cross-multiplication to solve for the unknown.

Step 1: Set up the equation:
$$\frac{AB}{BC} = \frac{DE}{EF}, \text{ or } \frac{9}{12} = \frac{15}{n}$$

Step 2: Calculate: $9n = 180$ $n = 20$

So side EF is 20 and side $DF = \sqrt{15^2 + 20^2}$
$= 25$

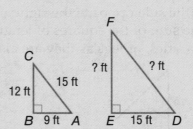

Exercises SOLVE

Find the missing sides of the following pairs of *similar* right triangles:

1 HI = _____ ft

 KL = _____ ft

 JL = _____ ft

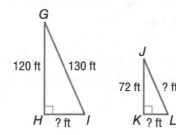

2 LN = _____ m

 PQ = _____ m

 OQ = _____ m

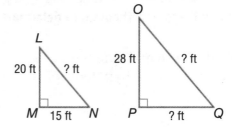

3 RT = _____ in.

 VW = _____ in.

 UW = _____ in.

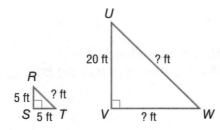

4 If the two triangles are similar, then what is the length of the missing side?

_____

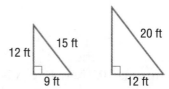

Name _____

Quadrilaterals

A 2-dimensional figure with four angles and four sides is called a **quadrilateral**. You can already recognize a **rectangle**, a 2-dimensional figure with four right angles. The opposite sides of a rectangle are parallel and the same length.

rectangle

If *all* four sides of a rectangle are the same length, it is a **square**.

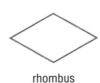
square

Like a rectangle, the opposite sides of a **rhombus** are parallel and all sides are the same length. However, unlike a rectangle, a rhombus does *not* have four right angles.

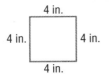
rhombus

A **trapezoid** has two opposite sides that are parallel, but the sides are *not* the same length. The other two sides of a trapezoid are *not* parallel.

trapezoid

If a quadrilateral looks like a typical toy kite, it is called a **kite**. Two of its angles are equal. Its longer two *touching* sides are equal in length, and so are its shorter two *touching* sides.

kite

Exercises   IDENTIFY

For each figure below, label as a square, rectangle, rhombus, trapezoid, or kite.

 4 in.
4 in. 4 in.
4 in.

❶ _____

B ____ C

A   D

❷ _____

❸ _____

b
a   a
b

❹ _____

❺ _____

❻ _____

❼ _____

❽ _____

❾ _____

Name _____

Polygons

Have you ever seen a 2-dimensional figure that has more than 4 sides? You have if you have seen a traffic sign. A stop sign is an octagon, an eight-sided **polygon**. A polygon is a closed 2-dimensional figure made up of line segments. In fact, triangles and quadrilaterals are polygons, too. However, mathematicians usually do not call a figure a polygon unless it has more than 3 sides. As you might have guessed, for each side there is also an angle. The most common polygons are named for the number of their sides.

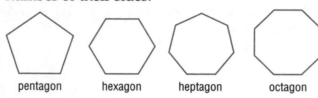

pentagon   hexagon   heptagon   octagon

penta = 5, **hexa** = 6, **hepta** = 7, **octa** = 8.

If two polygons have exactly the same shape, size, and angles, then they are congruent. Congruent polygons do *not* have to face in the same direction. So do *not* trust your eyes. The best way to tell if two polygons are congruent is to measure the sides and angles of both.

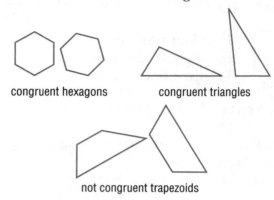

congruent hexagons   congruent triangles

not congruent trapezoids

To find the perimeter of a polygon, add the lengths of its sides.

Exercises   IDENTIFY

Indicate whether the figure is a polygon. Write "Polygon" or "Not a Polygon"

1 _____

2 _____

3 _____

4 _____

5 _____

6 _____

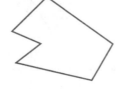

7 _____

8 _____

9 _____

Circles

Can you think of a closed 2-dimensional figure that has *no* angles? Did you think of a **circle**?

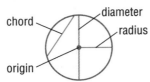

You need to know some special terms to describe circles. A circle's **circumference** is its perimeter, the distance around it. Every point on a circle's circumference is an equal distance from the circle's center point, or **origin**.

A **radius** is a line segment that begins at a circle's origin and extends to its circumference. In a circle, all radii (plural of "radius") are equal in length.

A line segment that has both of its endpoints on the circumference is called a **chord**. If a chord passes through the circle's origin, it is called a **diameter**. The length of a circle's diameter is two times the length of a circle's radius.

Exercises   SOLVE

1 What is the diameter of the circle?

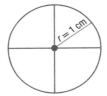

_____

2 What is the diameter of the circle?

_____

3 What is the radius of the circle below?

_____

4 What is the center of the circle?

_____

5 What is the radius of the circle?

_____

6 What are the two radii of the circle?

_____

Name _____

Circles (cont.)

Imagine that you want to find the length around a figure. Imagine that you want to find the circumference, or perimeter, of a circle, the distance around it. How can you measure that? And how can you find the area of a circle? A circle's circumference and area are calculated by using a special long decimal, written as the Greek letter π, pronounced **pi**. To make calculations easier, pi is often rounded to 3.14.

Pi is the ratio of a circle's diameter to its circumference—a ratio that is exactly the same for every circle.

Calculating the circumference and area of a circle is actually fairly easy to do. A circle's circumference = pi times its diameter (πd). A circle's area = pi times the square of its radius = πr^2.

Exercises   SOLVE

1

What is the area of the circle? _____

What is the circumference? _____

2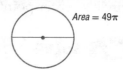

What is the circumference of the circle?

_____

What is the radius? _____

3

What is the diameter of the circle? _____

What is the area? _____

What is the circumference? _____

4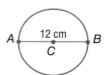

What is the circumference of the circle?

_____

What is the area of the circle? _____

5 A bicycle wheel measures 25 inches in diameter. How far would a bike travel if the wheel went completely around 4 times?

_____ inches

6 Brenda walks her dog along two circular routes laid out in the park. How much longer is Route B then route A? (Leave the answer in terms of pi.)

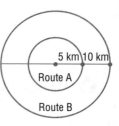

_____ π km

Name _____

Symmetry, Translation, Rotation, Projection

Symmetry is best illustrated by graphing a figure on a piece of paper, with a line going down the center. If you can fold the paper along that line and one half is identically sitting atop the other, then the figure is symmetrical. Every point on one side of the line has a matching point on the other side.

Line of symmetry

A **translation** occurs when you take a figure and make an identical duplicate of it. You can move the figure right or left and up or down.

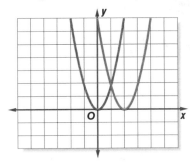

Rotation occurs when you move a figure around a point or a line. The shape remains the same, but its orientation, or the way it faces, changes.

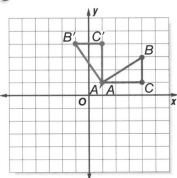

A person using an overhead projector to show an image from an overlay can alter the image's size by moving the screen further away or closer to the projector. In all other ways the projected image, or **projection**, is the same.

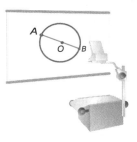

Exercises   **IDENTIFY**

For each pair of figures, label as symmetrical, translation, rotation, or projection.

❶ _____   ❷ _____

❸ _____   ❹ _____

Surface Area of Solid Figures

Not all figures are 2-dimensional. Can you name some common 3-dimensional, or solid, figures?

To describe **solid figures**, you need to know some special terms.

Face: A flat surface of a solid figure. Each face looks like a 2-dimensional figure.

Edge: The line at which two faces meet.

Vertex (of a Solid): A specific point at which *more than* 2 faces meet or where a curve originates.

Base: The face on the bottom of a solid figure.

Cube

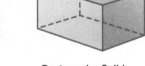
Rectangular Solid   Cylinder

Examples:

To find the surface area of a cube, or a rectangular solid, use the formula:
$2lw + 2lh + 2wh$

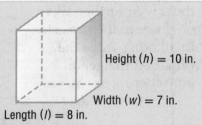
Height $(h) = 10$ in.
Width $(w) = 7$ in.
Length $(l) = 8$ in.

The surface area of the solid above is $(2 \times 8 \times 7) + (2 \times 8 \times 10) + (2 \times 7 \times 10) = 112 + 160 + 140 = 412$ **square inches**

To calculate the surface area of a cylinder, use the formula:
$2\pi r^2 + 2\pi rh$.

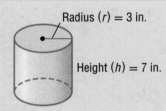
Radius $(r) = 3$ in.
Height $(h) = 7$ in.

The surface area of this cylinder
$= 2 \times \pi \times 3^2 + 2 \times \pi \times 3 \times 7 = 18\pi + 42\pi = 60\pi$ **square centimeters**.

Exercises   CALCULATE SURFACE AREA

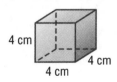
4 cm
4 cm
4 cm

1 _____

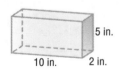
5 in.
10 in.   2 in.

2 _____

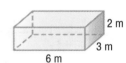
2 m
3 m
6 m

3 _____

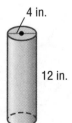
4 in.
12 in.

4 _____

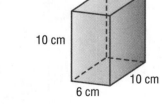
10 cm
6 cm   10 cm

5 _____

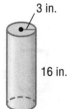
3 in.
16 in.

6 _____

Name _____

Volume of Solid Figures

You learned the units used to measure liquid volume in a container. However, what if you want to know a solid figure's **volume**, or how many units it contains? These units are called cubic inches, cubic feet, cubic yards, and cubic miles.

Example:

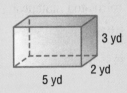

To find the volume of a rectangular solid, multiply length × width × height.

Volume = 5 yd × 2 yd × 3 yd = 30 cu yd

Example:

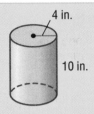

The volume of a cylinder can be calculated by using the formula $V = B \times h$ where the base $= \pi r^2$

$$Volume = \pi \times 4^2 \times 10$$
$$\pi \times 16 \times 10$$
$$160\pi$$

Exercises CALCULATE VOLUME

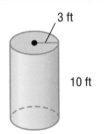

1 _____

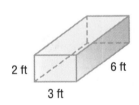

2 _____

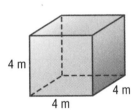

3 _____

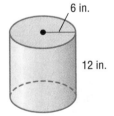

4 _____

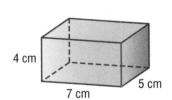

5 _____

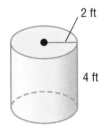

6 _____

Name _____

Volume of Solid Figures (cont.)

Examples:

The volume of a cone can be calculated by using the formula

$V = \frac{1}{3} \times$ base $\times$ height

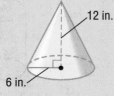

The base can be calculated with πr^2

Volume $= \frac{1}{3} \times \pi \times 6^2 \times 12$

$= \frac{1}{3} \times \pi \times 36 \times 12$

$= 144\pi$ cu in.

The volume of a rectangular pyramid is also calculated using the formula

$V = \frac{1}{3} \times b \times h$

The base can be calculated multiplying length × width.

Volume $= \frac{1}{3} \times 5$ ft $\times 5$ ft $\times 15$ ft

$= \frac{1}{3} \times 375$ cu ft

$= 125$ cu ft

Exercises   CALCULATE VOLUME

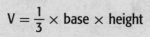

1 _____

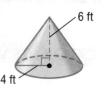

2 _____

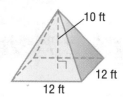

3 _____

4 _____

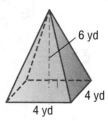

5 _____

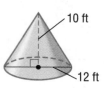 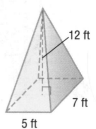 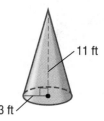

6 _____

Lessons 18–22

Identify each angle as obtuse, acute, or right.

1  135°

_____

2 90°

_____

3 45°

_____

Identify each pair of angles as supplementary, complementary, or neither, and explain why.

4

_____

_____

_____

5

_____

_____

_____

6

_____

_____

_____

Identify each triangle as scalene, equilateral, or isosceles.

7

_____

8

_____

9

_____

Identify each triangle as obtuse, right, or acute.

10

_____

11

_____

12

_____

13

Lessons 18–22

Identify the figures.

14 _____

15  _____

16 _____

17 _____

18 _____

Fill in the information for each figure.

19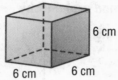
6 cm
6 cm   6 cm

Figure _____

Volume _____

Surface Area _____

20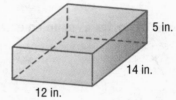
5 in.
14 in.
12 in.

Figure _____

Volume _____

Surface Area _____

21
4 ft
6 ft

Figure _____

Volume _____

22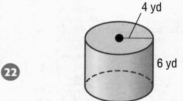
4 yd
6 yd

Figure _____

Volume _____

Surface Area _____

B C
D
H G
A

23 Name the center point.

_____

24 Which segments are chords?

_____

25 Which segment is the diameter?

_____

26 Which segments are radii?

_____

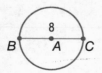
8
B A C

27 What is the circumference of the circle? (Use 3.14 as as a value for π).

_____

28 What is the area of the circle?

_____

Unit Test

Lessons 18–22

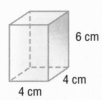
6 cm
4 cm
4 cm

29 Nathan bought a present for his sister Christine. It came in a box that looked like the figure shown here. Nathan wants to wrap the present before he gives it to his sister. How much wrapping paper does he need? _____

Use the Pythagorean Theorem to determine which triangles are right triangles. (Write Yes or No for each.)

30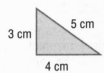
3 cm
5 cm
4 cm

_____

31
8 in.
10 in.
6 in.

_____

32
3 m
3 m
3 m

_____

33 Which two triangles are similar? _____

Are they congruent? _____

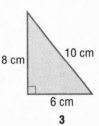
3 cm
3 cm
3√2 cm
1

4 in.
3 in.
5 in.
2

8 cm
6 cm
10 cm
3

34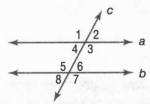
c
1 2
4 3
a
5 6
8 7
b

Identify all vertical angle pairs.

_____

Are angles 1 and 3 equal in measure?

_____

List four supplementary angle pairs.

_____

Identify an exterior angle pair. _____

Identify an interior angle pair. _____

35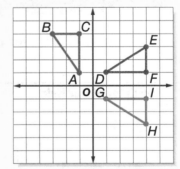

Which triangle is a rotation of triangle *ABC*?

_____

Which triangle is symmetrical to *DEF*?

_____

Bar Graphs

Graphs are useful ways to display information, or **data**. A **bar graph** uses bars to compare two or more people, places, or things. The bars may be horizontal or vertical. Each bar represents a number. Because the data are shown visually, the bars can be compared to one another. Sometimes different colored bars that represent different kinds of people or things are used.

Examples:

There are 78 students in the 8th grade at Jay County Middle School. Each student voted for his or her favorite kind of pie.

The key tells you which bars stand for girls and which bars stand for boys. The horizontal line, or **axis**, at the bottom of the graph names different kinds of pie.

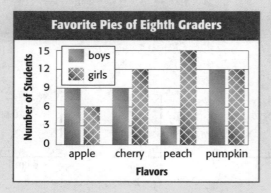

Favorite Pies of Eighth Graders

The vertical axis tells you how many boys and how many girls voted for their favorite pie.

How many students in total voted for either apple or peach pie?

Step 1: Find "apple" on the horizontal axis. Look at the top of each bar in the "apple" section, and follow that line back to the vertical axis to find out how many girls voted for apple pie, and how many boys voted for apple pie. 9 boys + 6 girls = 15 students in total voted for apple pie.

Step 2: Find "peach" on the horizontal axis. Repeat the process outlined in Step 1. 3 boys + 15 girls = 18 students.

Step 3: Add: 15 + 18 = 33 students voted for either peach or apple pie.

Exercises   INTERPRET

❶ On the bar graph, which hair color is the least common?

❷ In which two months did the company lose money?

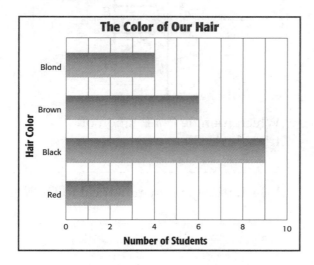

The Color of Our Hair

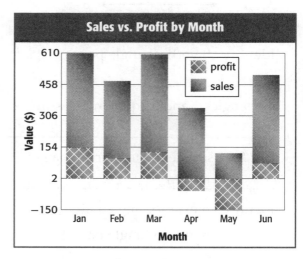

Sales vs. Profit by Month

3 What months had the most and least sales?

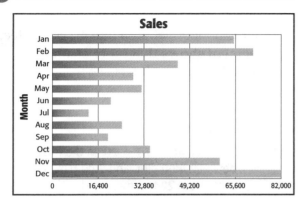

Most _____

Least _____

4 Which two people own the most pairs of shoes?

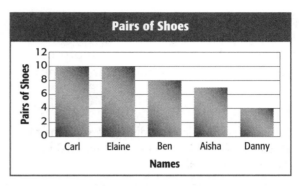

_____

5 Your friend constructed a bar graph to show which types of movies he watches most. Based on this information, what type of movie should you not bring to his house for viewing?

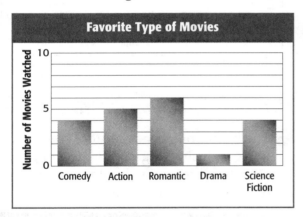

_____

6 Which mode of transportation had the most growth in passenger miles and which one had the least?

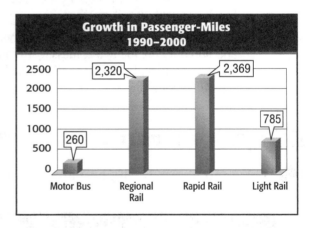

Most _____

Least _____

7 Write a sentence to summarize the trend illustrated in this graph showing park visitors.

_____

_____

_____

_____

_____

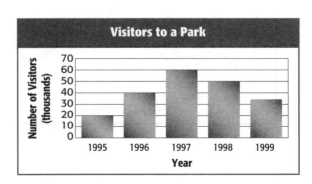

Name _____

Line Graphs

A **line graph** is often used to show how information changes as time passes. Each number on the horizontal axis represents a specific time. The distance from one time to another is an **interval**. In a line graph, a steeper line segment shows that more change has occurred during that interval.

Example:

During what time interval did Frank send the most text messages? About how many messages did he send during that interval?

Step 1: Look for the steepest line segment between intervals. That segment is between 4:00 p.m. and 7:00 p.m.

Step 2: Look along the horizontal axis for the time at the beginning of that interval. Then look at where the line is at that time on the vertical axis to find out how many text messages were sent by then. By 4:00 p.m., Frank had sent 20 text messages.

Step 3: Look for the time at the end of that interval and find out how many text messages Frank had sent by then. By 7:00 p.m., Frank had sent 40 messages.

Step 4: Subtract. 40 − 20 = 20. In the interval between 4:00 p.m. and 7:00 p.m., Frank sent about 20 text messages.

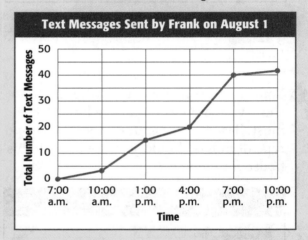

Exercises INTERPRET

❶ Which month has the highest amount of rainfall?

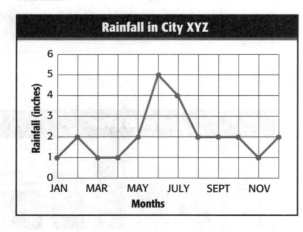

_____

_____

❷ The owner of a produce store studied this line graph showing potato consumption. On what three days should she make sure to have extra potatoes on hand?

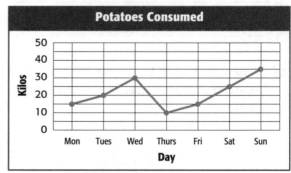

_____

_____

3 On which days would you expect usage of electricity to be the highest?

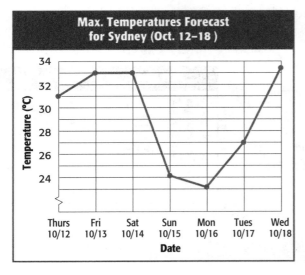

Max. Temperatures Forecast for Sydney (Oct. 12–18)

_____

_____

4 Summarize the trend displayed in this graph.

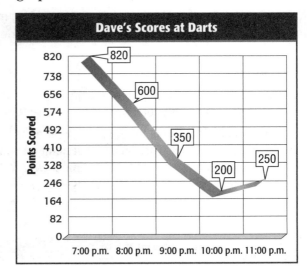

Dave's Scores at Darts

_____

_____

_____

5 Write a sentence summarizing the rapid decrease in value of a car.

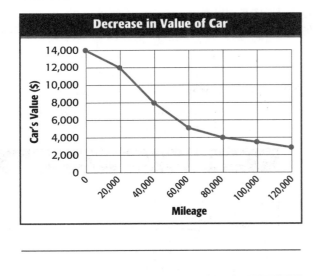

Decrease in Value of Car

_____

_____

_____

_____

_____

6 On which day did Caroline do the most driving?

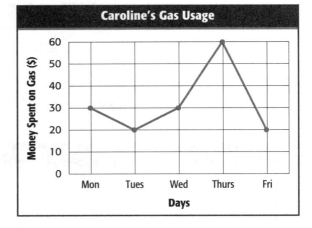

Caroline's Gas Usage

_____

_____

Double-Line Graphs

A **double-line graph** often compares how information changes
for two or more people, places, or things as time passes.

Example:

When had Amy and Jim both sent *exactly* the same total number
of messages? How many total messages were sent by each?

Step 1: Look for a point on the graph where the lines touch
one another. Then follow that point down to the
horizontal axis to see what time it was. At 10:00 p.m.,
they had each sent 50 messages.

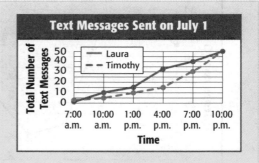

Exercises   **INTERPRET**

1 Which car is driving towards Taree?
Explain.

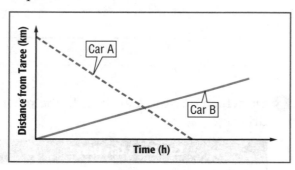

_____

2 Which of the two towns has a wider
variation in temperatures?

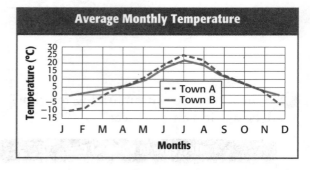

_____

3 Based on the double-line graph below, what
can you say happened in the year 2003?
Write a sentence summarizing the data.

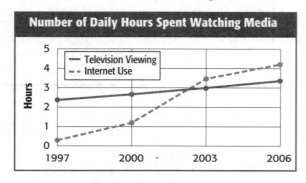

_____

_____

4 Write a sentence explaining what has
happened to urban and rural populations
in the U.S. since 1900.

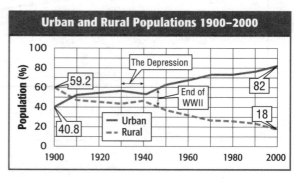

_____

_____

Circle Graphs

A **circle graph** compares parts, or segments, of a whole to the whole. Some people also call a circle graph a pie chart, because it looks like a pie that has been sliced. When you read a circle graph, you are comparing parts to each other and to the whole. However, sometimes you can calculate a part exactly.

Examples:

Which kind of coin did Olivia save most?

Step 1: Find the largest **segment** on the graph.

Step 2: Read the label for that segment. Olivia saved more quarters than any other kind of coin.

Olivia saved a total of 64 coins. How many of them were pennies?

Step 1: Look at the whole circle again. You may not be able to tell exactly how big each part is. However, you can estimate. If you compare pennies and dimes to the whole circle, those two **segments** account for half the circle.

Step 2: Multiply $\frac{1}{2} \times 64 = 32$. Altogether there are 32 pennies and dimes.

Step 3: Now compare the pennies and the dimes to each other. The segments look the same. So $\frac{1}{2}$ of those 32 coins are pennies and $\frac{1}{2}$ are dimes.

Step 4: Multiply $\frac{1}{2} \times 32 = 16$. There are 16 pennies.

Coins in Olivia's Bank

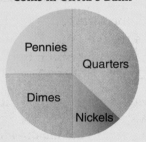

Exercises   INTERPRET

1 What are the three major areas of consumer expenditures?

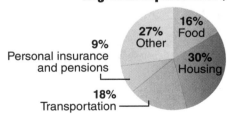

Consumer Expenditures
Avg. Total Expenditures: $29,846

16% Food
27% Other
9% Personal insurance and pensions
30% Housing
18% Transportation

_____

_____

2 Name the two regions that represent more than 50% of the company sales.

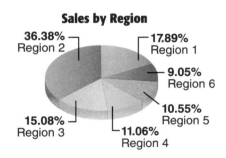

Sales by Region

36.38% Region 2
17.89% Region 1
9.05% Region 6
15.08% Region 3
11.06% Region 4
10.55% Region 5

_____

_____

Name _____

Measures of Central Tendency

Statistics is a branch of mathematics that studies data expressed as numbers. In the data, the numbers answer questions such as: How many? How long? How far? How big?

Suppose you have this group of numbers: 21, 10, 18, 10, 14, 7, 10, 14

Begin by arranging them in order: 7, 10, 10, 10, 14, 14, 18, 21

The **range** is the greatest number minus the smallest number. $21 - 7 = 14$

The **mean** (sometimes called the average) is the total of the whole collection divided by the number of addends. $104 \div 8 = 13$

The **median** is the number in the middle. If your collection has an even number of addends, the median is the average of the two middle ones. $(10 + 14) \div 2 = 24 \div 2 = 12$

The **mode** is the number that appears most frequently in the collection. In this example, the mode is 10.

Example:
Find the mean of 5, 3, 6, 10, 5, 2, 4

Step 1: Add the numbers.
$5 + 3 + 6 + 10 + 5 + 2 + 4 = 35$

Step 2: Divide by the number of addends.
$35 \div 7 = 5$

Remember...

The range, mean, median, and mode numbers *may* all be different! *Or* some of them *may* be identical.

Exercises   CALCULATE

Round all answers to the hundredths place.

1. 1, 2, 3, 4, 9, 8, 7, 6, 5   Mean ____ Median ____ Range ____ Mode ____

2. 10, 15, 20, 60, 110, 10, 10, 45   Mean ____ Median ____ Range ____ Mode ____

3. 23, 23, 24, 25, 48, 56, 32, 1, 2   Mean ____ Median ____ Range ____ Mode ____

4. 11, 22, 33, 44, 66, 77, 11, 21   Mean ____ Median ____ Range ____ Mode ____

5. 3, 3, 3, 3, 3, 4, 6, 7, 8   Mean ____ Median ____ Range ____ Mode ____

6. 4, 5, 6, 8, 9, 21, 22, 23, 24, 21, 5, 27   Mean ____ Median ____ Range ____ Mode ____

7. 9, 13, 56, 12, 13, 9, 9, 18, 45   Mean ____ Median ____ Range ____ Mode ____

8. −3, −10, −10, 14, 16, 22, 21, 30   Mean ____ Median ____ Range ____ Mode ____

9. −1, −1, −5, −6, −7, 10, 1, 14, 27 Mean ____ Median ____ Range ____ Mode ____

10. −10, −20, −20, 0, 10, 20, 20   Mean ____ Median ____ Range ____ Mode ____

Stem-and-Leaf Plots

A **stem-and-leaf plot** organizes data by the place value of digits. Think of it as a plant with stems. Each stem may have a different number of leaves.

Example:

Math Test Scores in Mrs. Castro's Class

Stems	Leaves
6	6 7 8
7	4 5 5
8	2 4 6 8 8
9	0 0 2 8

To read this, attach each leaf to its stem. In Mrs. Castro's class, the test scores were 66, 67, 68, 74, 75, 75, 82, 84, 86, 88, 88, 90, 90, 92, and 98.

To find the range in a stem-and-leaf plot, look at the first leaf on the first stem and the last leaf on the last stem. Add them and divide by two.

Range = $(66 + 98) \div 2 = 164 \div 2 = 82$

Exercises   INTERPRET

1 Make a list all of the points scored in the basketball games.

Points Scored in Basketball Games

Stem	Leaves
3	9
4	0 1 5 7 7 7 9
5	2 6 6 6

_____

_____

2 Make a list of the data shown below.

Stem	Leaf
12	0 5 8 8
13	0 1 2 4 6 7 9
14	1 2 3 5 5 9
15	
16	1 5

_____

_____

3 Using the stem-and-leaf plot, determine the median age of people at the family reunion, the range, and the mode of the ages.

Ages of People at the Family Reunion

Stem	Leaves
0	1 8 9
3	2 4 7
4	5
5	1 5
8	1

Median _____

Range _____

Mode _____

4 In a biology class, eight students collected shrubs for a study. The number of shrubs collected by the students were 4, 8, 12, 16, 21, 21, and 23. Make a stem-and-leaf plot of these numbers.

Shrubs Collected by Students

Stem	Leaf

24.3

Name _____

Box-and-Whisker Plots

A **box-and-whisker plot** looks at data to tell where most of the numbers lie. This type of plot shows the medians in the data.

Example:

You have recorded the heights, in inches, of the 13 children you baby-sit for, and arranged these numbers in order: 21, 23, 26, 30, 34, 34, 36, 36, 37, 38, 40, 48, 52.

The **lower extreme** is the lowest number in your data, 21. The **upper extreme** is the highest number in your data, 52. The median of all the numbers in the data is the middle number, 36.

The **lower quartile** is the median of the numbers below the median. $(26 + 30) \div 2 = 28$

The **upper quartile** is the median of the numbers above the median. $(38 + 40) \div 2 = 39$

You have four sections on your line of data: each relative to its quartile mark, and each quartile mark relative to the median. Each quartile contains $\frac{1}{4}$ of the data.

What's the range of the lowest quartile?

Step 1: Find the lower extreme and the lower quartile. 21 and 28

Step 2: Subtract the lower extreme from the lower quartile. $28 - 21 = 7$

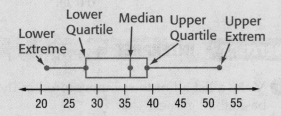

Exercises INTERPRET

1 Give the lower quartile for the box-and-whisker plot.

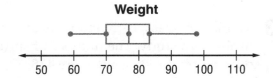

_____

2 What is the range for this box-and-whisker plot?

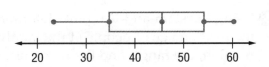

_____

3 Create a box-and-whisker plot from this information.

Summary	
Lower Extreme	5
Lower Quartile	8.5
Median	12
Upper Quartile	14
Upper Extreme	20

4 What is the range and median of this box-and-whisker plot?

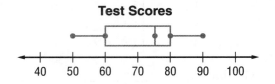

Range _____

Median _____

Tree Diagrams

A **tree diagram** can be used to show possible combinations of people, places, or things. It looks like a set of trees with branches.

Example:

At a community cookout, you can buy a ticket that allows you to choose one main item, and one side dish. The tree diagram shows the possible combinations.

To find out how many possible combinations there are, count the number of branches. In this example there are nine branches. How many possible combinations would there be if you could also order chips as a side dish?

Add potato chips as a branch on *each* main item. Since there are 3 items, add 9 + 3 = 12

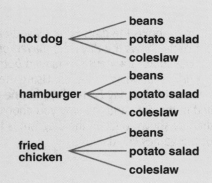

hot dog — beans, potato salad, coleslaw

hamburger — beans, potato salad, coleslaw

fried chicken — beans, potato salad, coleslaw

Exercises   DIAGRAM

1. Phil first rolls a 6-sided number cube then flips a coin. Draw a tree diagram that shows all the possible outcomes of Phil's actions. How many different outcomes are there?

   _____

   How many outcomes exist where Phil rolls an even number and he flips a coin "heads"?

   _____

2. Felicia is laying out her wardrobe for an upcoming vacation. She will be gone 4 days. She lays out 4 shirts (blue, black, red, yellow), 3 pairs of pants (black, tan, white), and 3 pairs of shoes (black, brown, red). Draw a tree diagram to show all of the different combinations of outfits that Felicia could wear on the trip. How many combinations are there?

   _____

   If Felicia brings only two pairs of shoes but adds another shirt, how many possible combinations will she have?

   _____

   Will she have more choices or fewer choices?

   _____

24.5

Venn Diagrams

A **Venn Diagram** is used to show *groups* of data and can also show if and when some of the data is placed in more than one group.

Example:

The left circle shows the days Edna played *only* Baseball Blaster. The right circle shows the days she played *only* Football Fun. The overlap area shows the days she played *both* games. Some data does not fit into the diagram at all. Using the data shown in this diagram, identify the day Edna played none of the games identified in the data and tell why you choose that day. In this case, the day shown outside the diagram is the day Edna played none of the games listed.

Games Played by Edna in a Week

Exercises **DIAGRAM**

1 Ramon surveyed a group of 50 people at the town meeting about the expansion of the town zoo and the construction of a bike path. He found that of the 50 people he surveyed, 32 people supported expanding the zoo and 30 people supported constructing a bike path. Twelve people supported both projects. Fill in the Venn Diagram to represent the results of the survey.

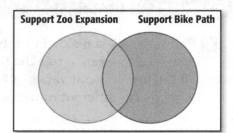

How many people supported the town zoo only? _____

How many supported the bike path only? _____

2 The manager of the local clothing store wants to know which jeans to stock for the upcoming back-to-school sale. He reviews the numbers from last year's sale and finds that the store sold 120 pairs of jeans. 80 were boot-cut, and 60 were stone-washed. Assuming the store only stocked those two styles of jeans, how many of the jeans sold were both stone-washed and boot-cut?

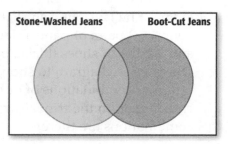

_____

How many of the jeans were just stone-washed and not boot-cut? _____

How many were just boot-cut and not stone-washed? _____

Complete the Venn Diagram to show the data.

Calculating Probabilities

Probability is the likelihood of something happening in the future. Knowing how to calculate probability will help you predict future events, although not with 100 percent accuracy!

The simple formula to figure probability (*P*) is the number of favorable outcomes (*f*) divided by the total number of possible outcomes (*o*). You could express this formula as an equation.

$$P = \frac{f}{o}$$

Remember...

Probability only shows what is most likely to happen, not what will *definitely* happen. It is certainly possible that a person could throw a 6-sided number cube and that three fives, or 30 fives, or indeed 300 fives in a row would show—although the probability is great that this would not happen!

Example:

If you roll a 6-sided number cube, there are six possible outcomes. Each side has a different number of spots. The cube could show 1, 2, 3, 4, 5, or 6 spots.

What is the probability of the side with four spots being on top after the cube is thrown? The probability of rolling a 4 is $\frac{1}{6}$

What is the probability of a 5 or a 6 not being on top after a cube is thrown?

Step 1: Decide how many favorable outcomes there are. In this case $6 - 2 = 4$

Step 2: Set up your equation. $P = \frac{4}{6}$

Step 3: You could simplify that fraction. $\frac{4}{6} = \frac{2}{3}$

If you were to roll the cube three times, you would probably have a favorable outcome two of those times.

Exercises   INTERPRET

1 If you place 14 marbles in a bag with 7 red, 4 orange, and 3 black, what is the probability of blindly pulling a red marble from the bag?

_____

2 If there are 20 males and 15 females in your class, and the teacher wants to appoint one person to be in charge of attendance, what is the probability that this person will be a female?

_____

3 A survey was taken at school and all 525 students were asked if they belonged to a club. 212 people responded that they did belong to a club. What is the probability that if you randomly chose a person walking down the hall, that this person would belong to a club?

_____

4 Someone mistakenly put three boxes of hardboiled eggs in with the regular farm eggs that totaled 156 boxes. What is the probability that someone buying a box of eggs will get a box of hardboiled eggs?

_____

Lessons 23–24

1 What is the probability of:

Spinning an odd number? _____

Spinning a 2? _____

Spinning either a 2 or 4? _____

Spinning a 1? _____

2 What is the range of the data?

_____

What is the median of the data?

_____

What is the mean of the data?

_____

Stem-and-Leaf Plot	
4	5 6
5	6 8
6	1 7
7	2 7 8
8	9
9	4

3 How many different combinations of outfits can be created from the choices?

_____

How many possibilities are there that include green-striped shirts?

_____

How many possibilities are there that include a yellow tie and grey pants?

_____

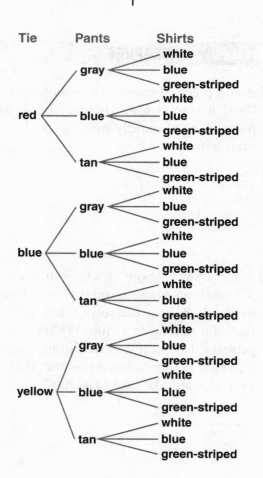

Unit Test

Lessons 23–24

4 What is the median of this data plot?

_____

What is the range of the data?

_____

Weight of Pet Cats (kg)

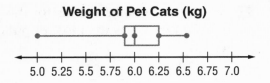

5.0 5.25 5.5 5.75 6.0 6.25 6.5 6.75 7.0

5 Students in James's health class were polled on their favorite health food snack. The results are displayed on the graph.

What is the least favorite health food snack?

_____

What is the favorite health food snack?

_____

How many more people preferred carrots to cauliflower?

_____

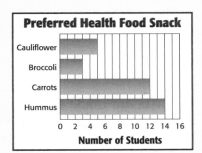

Preferred Health Food Snack

Cauliflower
Broccoli
Carrots
Hummus

0 2 4 6 8 10 12 14 16
Number of Students

6 Janice was making a schedule to determine how many volunteers she needed for the nature center guided tours. She charted the number of visitors to the nature center during the prior summer.

What month had the most visitors?

_____

What month had the fewest visitors?

_____

During what months should Janice increase her staffing to meet the demand for guided tours?

_____

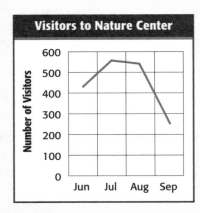

Visitors to Nature Center

Number of Visitors

600
500
400
300
200
100
0

Jun   Jul   Aug   Sep

Lessons 23–24

7 Peggy charted bike rentals for the previous month. What was the most popular kind of bike rented?

_____

Which kind of bike speed was the least popular?

_____

Bike Rentals

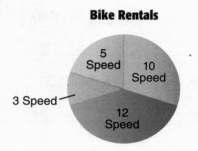

8 Coach Taylor made a chart of the performance of his two best hitters. In which month did Langely hit more extra base hits than Stanton?

_____

How many more extra base hits did Stanton have than Langely in the month of September?

_____

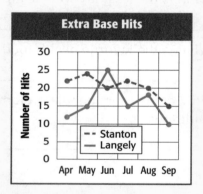

9 Use the Venn Diagram to display the following data: 25 students take Algebra I, 22 students take US History, and 8 students take both courses.

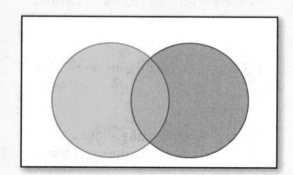

Posttest

Complete the following test items.

1 Robin runs 24 kilometers a week. If she continues to run at this rate, how many kilometers will she run in a year? _____

2 The fashion department at an outlet store had a sale on t-shirts. There were 1,124 t-shirts in stock at the beginning of the sale and another 426 more were ordered. At the end of the sale the store still had 335 t-shirts in stock. How many t-shirts were sold during the sale? _____

3 Ronnie has 12 lengths of garden hose. Each is $6\frac{3}{4}$ meters long.

How many meters of garden hose does Ronnie have to divide among 6 people working in the community garden? _____

How much hose will each person receive? _____

4 Don has 112 quarts of tomato sauce to divide among the 12 contestants in a pasta cooking contest. How many cups is that per contestant? _____

5 $6\frac{5}{8} + 3\frac{1}{4} + \frac{1}{6} + 1\frac{1}{3} =$

_____

6 $-10 + 15 - (-6) + 5(-4) + \frac{16}{-8} =$

_____

7 Solve for x: $x - 8 = 16$

_____

8 Solve for x: $3x + 6 = 30$

_____

9 Solve: $12 + (11 - 7)^2 - (16 \div 2) + 4(8 \times 2) - 3(8 - 2) =$ _____

10 Restate in exponent form, then solve: $4 \times 4 \times 4 \times 3 \times 3 + 5 \times 5 =$

_____

11 4.65 meters = _____ inches
(Use 2.54 cm = 1 inch)

12 16 yards = _____ centimeters

13 What is the area of the rectangle?

_____

What is the perimeter of the rectangle?

_____

15 cm

5 cm

14 What is the area of the circle? (Use 3.14 for π.)

8 in.

B   A   C

_____

What is the circumference of the circle?

_____

Name _____

15 Identify each angle as obtuse, acute, or right.

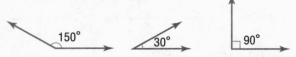

_____   _____   _____

16 Identify each triangle as scalene, isosceles, or equilateral.

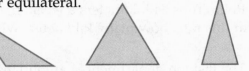

_____   _____   _____

Calculate and reduce the fractions.

17 $\dfrac{5}{12} \times 168 =$ _____

18 $\left(\dfrac{1}{3} \times \dfrac{9}{14}\right) \times \dfrac{14}{3} =$ _____

19 $\dfrac{56}{65} \div 14 =$ _____

20 Give the coordinates for points on the grid.

A _____   B _____

C _____   D _____

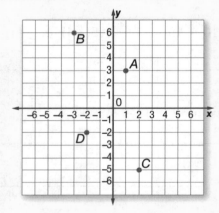

21 What is the measure of angle DBC?

_____

22 $.35\overline{)\,.595}$

23 $3\overline{)\,.5596}$

24 What is 30% of .802?

_____

25 What is $\dfrac{3}{8}$ of 96%?

_____

26 Restate 5.625 as an improper fraction and a mixed number.

Improper Fraction _____   Mixed Number _____

27 Put the following numbers in order from least to greatest.
2.356, 1.3561, 3.56302, 2.5631, 2.35692, 1.35688, 2.5622, 1.599

_____

28 Solve for x. $\dfrac{45}{64} = \dfrac{x}{192}$ _____

29 Restate $2\dfrac{7}{25}$ as a decimal. _____

30 An item costs you $13.50 to produce. What price would you charge if you wanted to mark up the item by 20%?

_____

31 Darma deposits $500 in a bank account that earns 2.5% simple interest. How much money will she have in the account after 1 year? _____

After 2 years? _____

32 Identify each quadrilateral.

_____ _____ _____ _____ _____

33 Restate $4\frac{11}{13}$ as an improper fraction.

_____

34 Restate $\frac{73}{13}$ as a mixed number.

_____

35 $\frac{6}{7} - \frac{2}{7} + \frac{5}{7} + \frac{3}{7} - \frac{1}{7} =$ _____

36 $\frac{15}{16} \times 3\frac{1}{5} =$ _____

37 $10^7 \times 10^2 =$ _____

38 $4^6 \div 4^3 =$ _____

39 What is 15^2? _____

40 What is the square root of 169?

_____

41 What is the mode of the data distribution?

_____

What is the median?

_____

3	2 3
4	2 3 6 8
5	4 7 7 7
6	1 2 4 4 6
7	1 4

42 What is the range of the data in the box-and-whisker plot?

_____

43 What fruit is the least preferred by the students? _____
What is the second most preferred fruit? _____

Favorite Fruit

Pineapple — Blueberry
Strawberry Banana

44 Clarence collected about 5 more stamps than what person? _____
Who collected the second fewest stamps? _____

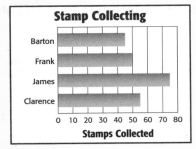

Stamp Collecting

Barton
Frank
James
Clarence

0 10 20 30 40 50 60 70 80
Stamps Collected

45 How many possible combinations are there?

_____

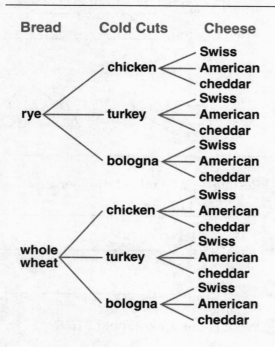

Bread	Cold Cuts	Cheese

chicken — Swiss, American, cheddar

rye — turkey — Swiss, American, cheddar

bologna — Swiss, American, cheddar

chicken — Swiss, American, cheddar

whole wheat — turkey — Swiss, American, cheddar

bologna — Swiss, American, cheddar

46

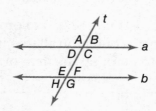

Name two pairs of alternate interior angles.

_____ and _____

_____ and _____

Name two pairs of alternate exterior angles.

_____ and _____

_____ and _____

Name a pair of vertical angles.

_____ and _____

Name two pairs of supplementary angles.

_____ and _____

_____ and _____

47 Use the Pythagorean Theorem to find the value of x. _____

48 Name 2 line segments. _____

Name 4 rays. _____

Name a line. _____

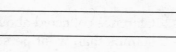
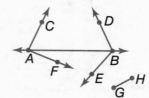

Calculate the volume and surface area of the figures shown.

49

Volume _____

Surface Area _____

50

Volume _____

Surface Area _____

51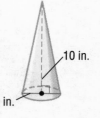

Volume _____

Acute Angle: An angle with a measure of less than 90°. *(p. 99)*

Acute Triangle: A triangle with only acute angles, angles less than 90°. *(p. 103)*

Addend: Any number that is added to another number. *(p. 8)*

Algebraic Expression: A group of letters, numbers, and symbols used in a series of operations. *(p. 69)*

Angle: Two rays that share an endpoint. *(p. 99)*

Area: The measure of a 2- or 3-dimensional figure's interior, given in square units. *(p. 86)*

Associative Property of Addition: States that addends may be grouped in any order without changing the sum. *(p. 60)*

Associative Property of Multiplication: States that numbers may be grouped in any way without changing the product. *(p. 60)*

Bar Graph: A graph that uses numbers to compare two or more people, places, or things. Each bar represents a number and may be represented horizontally or vertically. *(p. 118)*

Base: The face on the bottom of a solid figure. *(p. 112)*

Base of an Exponent: The number being used as the factor when writing in exponential form. In the statement 10^3, the base is 10. *(p. 54)*

Box-and-Whisker Plot: Organizes data to show where the most data points lie and also shows the median of the data. *(p. 126)*

Carry: To place an extra digit—when adding or multiplying—in the next place-value column on the left. *(p. 8)*

Celsius: Used in the metric system to measure temperature and expressed as °C, also expressed as Centigrade. *(p. 93)*

Chord: A line segment with both endpoints on a circle's circumference. *(p. 109)*

Circle: A 2-dimensional figure with every point on its circumference an equal distance from its center point. *(p. 109)*

Circle Graph: Shows parts of a whole as a percentage to the whole and is also known as a pie chart. *(p. 123)*

Circumference: The length of distance around a circle's perimeter. *(p. 109)*

Coefficient: The number that replaces the symbol × and multiplies the variable in a multiplication expression. The statement $9m$ shows 9 as the coefficient and m as the variable. *(p. 69)*

Common Denominator: A number which can be divided evenly by all the denominators in a group of fractions. *(p. 18)*

Commutative Property of Additions: States that numbers may be added in any order without changing the sum. *(p. 60)*

Commutative Property of Multiplication: States that multiplication may be done in any order without changing the product. *(p. 60)*

Compatible Numbers: Numbers that are easy to work with in your head. *(p. 18)*

Complementary Angles: Two angles that form a right angle. Their sum is 90°. *(p. 100)*

Congruent: A term used to describe something that is equal. *(p. 103)*

Cross-multiplying: A method for finding a missing numerator or denominator. *(p. 31)*

Customary Units of Length: Measurements expressed in inches (*in.*), feet (*ft*), yards (*yd*), and miles (*mi*). *(p. 82)*

Customary Units of Weight: Measurements expressed in ounces (*oz*), pounds (*lb*), and tons. *(p. 84)*

Cylinder: A three-dimensional figure with two parallel and congruent circular bases and one curved surface. *(p. 112)*

Data: Information that is gathered and sometimes displayed in graphs and charts. *(p. 118)*

Denominator: The number below the line in a fraction. *(p. 14)*

Diameter: A chord that passes through a circle's center point. *(p. 109)*

Discount: A reduction in the cost of an item from the usual price. *(p. 34)*

Distributive Property of Multiplication: States that each number may be multiplied separately and added together. *(p. 61)*

Dividend: The number to be divided in a division problem. *(p. 12)*

Divisor: The number by which another number—the dividend—will be divided. *(p. 12)*

Double-Line Graph: Compares how information changes as time passes between two or more people, places, or things. *(p. 122)*

Edge: The line on a solid figure where two faces meet. *(p. 112)*

Equality Property of Addition: States that when adding a number on one side of an equation, you must add the same number on the other side of an equation. Both sides will then still be equal. *(p. 62)*

Equality Property of Division: States that when dividing a number on one side of an equation, you must divide by the same number on the other side of the equation. Both sides will then still be equal. *(p. 62)*

Equality Property of Multiplication: States that when multiplying a number on one side of an equation, you must multiply by the same number on the other side of the equation. Both sides will then still be equal. *(p. 62)*

Equality Property of Subtraction: States that when subtracting a number on one side of an equation, you must subtract the same number on the other side of the equation. Both sides will then still be equal. *(p. 62)*

Equation: A mathematical statement used to show that two amounts are equal. *(p. 31)*

Equilateral Triangle: A triangle with all three sides being the same length. *(p. 103)*

Exponent: The number that tells how many times the base number is multiplied by itself. The exponent ^{3} in 10^3 shows $10 \times 10 \times 10$. *(p. 54)*

Exterior Angle: An angle located outside parallel lines when a line intersects the parallel lines. *(p. 100)*

Face: The flat surface of a solid figure. On a solid figure each face looks two-dimensional. *(p. 112)*

Factors: The numbers multiplied in a multiplication exercise. *(p. 49)*

Fahrenheit: The customary system used to measure temperature and expressed as °F. *(p. 93)*

First Power: In an exponent, a base raised to the first power equals the base. *(p. 86)*

Function Table: Used to show a relation between an ordered pair. *(p. 75)*

Hypotenuse: The side opposite the right angle on a right triangle. *(p. 105)*

Identity Elements: Numbers in a problem that do not affect the answer. Only addition and multiplication have identity elements. *(p. 61)*

Improper Fraction: A fraction greater than 1 because its numerator is greater than its denominator. *(p. 14)*

Interest: The percent of the principal charged by the bank for money borrowed, or paid to a person with money in a savings account. *(p. 38)*

Interior Angle: An angle located inside parallel lines when a line intersects the parallel lines. *(p. 100)*

Intersecting Lines: Lines that meet or cross each other at a specific point. *(p. 97)*

Interval: The distance between each measurement of time on a line graph. *(p. 120)*

Inverse: A number's exact opposite on the other side of the number line. The inverse of −9 is 9. *(p. 66)*

Irrational Number: The square root of a number that is not a perfect square. *(p. 57)*

Isosceles Triangle: A triangle with two sides the same length, but the third side being a different length. *(p. 103)*

Kite: A quadrilateral with two angles that are equal, two touching sides that are equal in length, and the other two touching sides are equal in length. *(p. 107)*

Like Denominators: Fractions that have the same denominator. *(p. 16)*

Line: A straight path that goes in both directions and does not end. A line is measured in length. *(p. 97)*

Line Graph: Often used to show a change in information as time passes. The distance from one time to another is an interval. *(p. 120)*

Line Segment: A specific part of a line that ends at two identified points. *(p. 98)*

Liquid Volume: Units of liquid a container can hold and expressed in cups (*c*), pints (*pt*), quarts (*qt*), and gallons (*gal*). *(p. 83)*

Lower Extreme: The lowest number in a group of data used in a box-and-whisker plot. *(p. 126)*

Lower Quartile: The median of numbers from the lower extreme to the median on a box-and-whisker plot. *(p. 126)*

Glossary

Mark-up: The percent by which something is increased before it is sold. (p. 34)

Mean: The total number of the whole collection divided by the number of addends. (p. 124)

Median: The middle number in a set of numbers when the numbers are arranged from least to greatest. (p. 124)

Metric Units of Length: Measurements expressed in millimeters (*mm*), centimeters (*cm*), meters (*m*), and kilometers (*km*). (p. 87)

Metric Units of Liquid Volume: Measurements expressed in liter (*L*), milliliters (*mL*), centiliters (*cL*), and kiloliters (*kL*). (p. 88)

Metric Units of Mass: Measurements expressed in grams (*g*), milligrams (*mg*), centigrams (*cg*), and kilograms (*kg*). (p. 112)

Mixed Number: A number with a whole number part and a fraction part. (p. 14)

Mode: The number that appears most often in a set of numbers. (p. 124)

Negative Exponent: A negative exponent creates a fraction. (p. 56)

Negative Number: A number less than 0 and identified with the minus sign. (p. 63)

Numerator: The number above the line in a fraction. (p. 14)

Obtuse Angle: An angle with a measure of more than 90°. (p. 99)

Obtuse Triangle: A triangle with one obtuse angle. (p. 103)

Order of Operations: Rules that tell the steps to follow when doing a computation. (p. 59)

Ordered Pair: Numbers used to identify a point on a grid. (p. 73)

Origin of a Circle: The circle's center point. (p. 109)

Percent: A special ratio that compares a number to 100 using the % symbol. (p. 33)

Percent Change: The amount of change from a starting point. (p. 34)

Perfect Square: Numbers that result from squaring an integer. (p. 57)

Perimeter: The distance around a figure. Measured in customary or metric units. (p. 85)

Pi: The ratio of a circle's diameter to its circumference—a ratio that is exactly the same for every circle. A circle's circumference equals pi times its diameter. A circle's area equals pi times the square of its radius. Pi is often rounded to 3.14. (p. 110)

Place Value: The value of a position of a digit in a number. (p. 43)

Point: An exact location in space that has no dimensions and cannot be measured. A point is usually represented by a dot. (p. 97)

Polygon: Any closed two-dimensional figure that is made up of line segments. Triangles and quadrilaterals are two types of polygons. (p. 108)

Power of 10: In a place-value chart, each place value is 10 times the place value of the number to its right. (p. 54)

Principal: The amount borrowed or deposited into a bank. (p. 38)

Probability: The likelihood of an event happening in the future. (p. 129)

Product: The result, or answer, of a multiplication problem. (p. 11)

Projection: Altering the size of an image by moving a projector closer or further away from a screen. (p. 111)

Property of Additive Inverses: States that when adding a negative number to its inverse the sum will be 0. For example: $-8 + 8 = 0$. (p. 66)

Proportion: An equation that shows two ratios are equal. (p. 31)

Pythagorean Theorem: In a right triangle, the square of the length of the hypotenuse is equal to the sum of the squares of the lengths of the other two sides. (p. 105)

Quadrilateral: A two-dimensional figure with four sides and four angles. (p. 107)

Quotient: The result of dividing one number by another. (p. 12)

Radical Sign: The symbol used to indicate a square root. (p. 57)

Radius: A line segment that starts at a circle's center point and extends to its perimeter. (p. 109)

Range: The greatest number minus the smallest number in a set of numbers. (p. 124)

Rate: A comparison of two different units or numbers. (p. 32)

Ratio: A comparison of two numbers using division. (p. 30)

Ray: A part of a line that extends from a specific point in only one direction. (p. 98)

Reciprocals: Two fractions that look like upside-down reflections of one another. (p. 23)

Rectangle: A quadrilateral with four right angles. A rectangle's opposite sides are parallel and the same length. (p. 107)

Reducing: The act of changing a fraction to its simplest form. (p. 21)

Regroup: In place value, to use part of the value from one place in another place to make adding or subtracting possible. (p. 9)

Remainder: The number left over in whole-number division when you can no longer divide any further. (p. 12)

Rhombus: A quadrilateral having four equal sides with opposite sides parallel. (p. 107)

Right Angle: An angle that measures exactly 90°. (p. 99)

Right Triangle: A triangle with one right angle, an angle with a measure of exactly 90°. (p. 103)

Rotation: Occurs when a figure is moved around a point or line. The shape remains the same but the orientation changes. (p. 111)

Rounding: To drop or zero-out digits in a number to a higher or lower value. (p. 43)

Rounding Place: The highest place value used in rounding. (p. 43)

Scalene Triangle: A triangle with all three sides being of different lengths. (p. 103)

Scientific Notation: A way of writing numbers as the product of a power of 10 and a decimal that is greater than 1 but less than 10. (p. 58)

Similar Traingles: Triangles with the same shape but with different sizes. (p. 104)

Solid Figure: A three-dimensional figure such as a cube or pyramid. (p. 112)

Square: A quadrilateral with four right angles and four sides that are the same length. (p. 107)

Square Root: A number that when multiplied by itself equals a given number. (p. 57)

Statistics: A branch of math that answers questions about how many, how long, how often, how far, or how big. (p. 124)

Stem-and-Leaf Plot: Used to organize data and compare it. A stem-and-leaf plot organizes data from least to greatest using the digits or the greatest place value to group data. (p. 125)

Supplementary Angles: Any two angles that add up to a sum of 180°. (p. 100)

Symmetry: Results when a figure is folded down the center and the parts are identical. (p. 111)

Translation: Occurs when an identical figure is drawn and then moved in any direction. (p. 111)

Tree Diagram: Used to show possible combinations of data including people, places, or things in a diagram that looks like a tree with branches. (p. 127)

Trapezoid: A quadrilateral that has two sides that are parallel to each other and two sides that are not parallel. (p. 107)

Triangle: A two-dimensional figure with three sides. (p. 103)

Upper Extreme: The highest number in a group of data used in a box-and-whisker plot. (p. 126)

Upper Quartile: The median of the numbers from the median to the upper extreme on a box-and-whisker plot. (p. 126)

Variable: An unknown number usually expressed as a letter and used in Algebra. In the statement $n - 18$, n is the variable. (p. 69)

Venn Diagram: A diagram used to show data and how different sets of data can overlap. (p. 128)

Vertex: The specific point of a ray, also called an endpoint. (p. 98)

Vertex of a Solid: A specific point at which more than two faces meet, or a point where a curve begins. (p. 112)

Vertical Angles: The angles opposite each other when two lines intersect. (p. 100)

Volume: The number of units a solid figure contains, expressed in cubic inches, feet, yards, or miles. (p. 113)

Whole Number: A number that does not include a fraction or decimal. (p. 8)

Zero Power: In an exponent, a base raised to the zero power equals 1. (p. 54)

Zero Property of Multiplication: States that any number times zero equals zero. (p. 62)

Answers

Lesson 3.5 (cont.)

1. $6\frac{101}{117}$

2. $3\frac{1}{30}$

3. $1\frac{1}{2}$

4. $9\frac{11}{36}$

5. $10\frac{5}{42}$

6. $4\frac{19}{55}$

7. $9\frac{19}{22}$

8. $\frac{8}{9}$

9. $36\frac{2}{51}$

10. $6\frac{1}{2}$

11. $19\frac{19}{40}$

12. $12\frac{19}{21}$

Lesson 3.6

1. $\frac{2}{5}$

2. $\frac{1}{12}$

3. $\frac{5}{18}$

4. $\frac{3}{55}$

5. $\frac{4}{25}$

6. $\frac{3}{91}$

7. $\frac{5}{14}$

8. $\frac{22}{65}$

9. $\frac{1}{6}$

10. $\frac{21}{55}$

11. $\frac{39}{68}$

12. $\frac{343}{1000}$

13. $\frac{2}{3}$

14. $\frac{1}{8}$

15. $\frac{12}{55}$

16. $\frac{91}{256}$

Lesson 4.1

1. $3\frac{1}{4}$

2. $4\frac{2}{7}$

3. $8\frac{1}{4}$

4. 18

5. $6\frac{3}{10}$

6. $3\frac{11}{17}$

7. $1\frac{3}{4}$

8. $12\frac{8}{11}$

9. $2\frac{2}{9}$

10. $4\frac{2}{3}$

11. $9\frac{3}{5}$

12. $5\frac{1}{2}$

13. $37\frac{5}{7}$

14. $11\frac{1}{2}$

15. 18

16. $8\frac{8}{9}$

17. $17\frac{1}{2}$ gallons

18. $10\frac{2}{7}$ hours

Lesson 4.2

1. $\frac{2}{3}$

2. $\frac{2}{9}$

3. $\frac{6}{35}$

4. $\frac{1}{4}$

5. $\frac{1}{2}$

6. $\frac{4}{7}$

7. $\frac{1}{10}$

8. $\frac{1}{8}$

9. $\frac{1}{2}$

10. $\frac{2}{3}$

11. $\frac{4}{225}$

12. $\frac{1}{5}$

13. $1\frac{1}{2}$

14. $\frac{1}{2}$

15. $\frac{3}{10}$

16. $\frac{4}{9}$

17. $\frac{5}{64}$ miles

18. $1\frac{2}{9}$ gallons

Lesson 4.3

1. $\frac{3}{4}$

2. $\frac{5}{12}$

3. $3\frac{1}{2}$

4. 4

5. $1\frac{1}{2}$

6. 3

7. $1\frac{1}{5}$

8. 1

9. 4

10. 1

11. $\frac{2}{3}$

12. $1\frac{1}{5}$

13. $1\frac{3}{4}$

14. $\frac{4}{5}$

15. $\frac{27}{40}$

16. 2

17. $15\frac{3}{10}$ yards

18. $2\frac{1}{4}$ hours

Answers

Lesson 4.4

1. $20\frac{5}{8}$
2. $6\frac{8}{15}$
3. $25\frac{27}{35}$
4. $21\frac{7}{12}$
5. $11\frac{2}{3}$
6. $9\frac{23}{28}$
7. $74\frac{2}{3}$
8. $49\frac{2}{5}$
9. 12
10. $30\frac{5}{8}$
11. $19\frac{1}{32}$
12. 21
13. $6\frac{18}{25}$
14. $22\frac{32}{55}$
15. $36\frac{4}{45}$
16. $40\frac{1}{28}$

Lesson 5.1

1. $\frac{3}{8}$
2. $\frac{3}{32}$
3. $\frac{2}{27}$
4. $\frac{1}{48}$
5. $\frac{9}{57}$ or $\frac{3}{19}$
6. $\frac{2}{15}$
7. $\frac{4}{81}$
8. $\frac{1}{18}$
9. $\frac{2}{11}$
10. $\frac{5}{19}$
11. $\frac{2}{31}$
12. $\frac{11}{252}$
13. $\frac{1}{159}$
14. $\frac{1}{42}$
15. $\frac{3}{31}$
16. $\frac{4}{63}$
17. $\frac{3}{32}$ pounds each
18. $\frac{6}{25}$ yards

Lesson 5.2

1. 50
2. 15
3. 16
4. 27
5. 16
6. 54
7. 72
8. 84
9. 40
10. $13\frac{1}{3}$
11. 28
12. 143
13. 55
14. 8
15. 99
16. 88
17. 225 packages
18. 25 stops

Lesson 5.3

1. $\frac{16}{7}$
2. $\frac{16}{7}$
3. $\frac{14}{27}$
4. 2
5. $\frac{9}{13}$
6. $\frac{49}{9}$
7. $\frac{3}{13}$
8. $\frac{5}{2}$
9. $\frac{16}{5}$
10. $\frac{3}{8}$
11. $\frac{42}{121}$
12. $\frac{1}{2}$

13. $\frac{9}{22}$
14. 3
15. $\frac{3}{2}$
16. $\frac{9}{25}$
17. 14 muffins
18. $7\frac{1}{2}$ miles

Lessons 5.4

1. $1\frac{5}{14}$
2. $1\frac{59}{189}$
3. $2\frac{1}{28}$
4. $1\frac{122}{207}$
5. $2\frac{1}{18}$
6. $1\frac{3}{4}$
7. $1\frac{2}{29}$
8. $\frac{74}{121}$
9. $1\frac{73}{104}$
10. $2\frac{30}{169}$
11. $\frac{117}{140}$
12. $1\frac{14}{15}$
13. $\frac{54}{91}$
14. $2\frac{3}{5}$
15. $4\frac{2}{9}$
16. $\frac{7}{18}$
17. $2\frac{1}{7}$ miles per hour
18. $5\frac{17}{20}$ pounds

Answers

Lesson 6.1

1. True
2. True
3. True
4. True
5. True
6. False
7. False
8. True
9. $\dfrac{5 \text{ plaster}}{4 \text{ water}}$
10. $\dfrac{3 \text{ pillowcases}}{2 \text{ sheets}}$
11. $\dfrac{2 \text{ forks}}{1 \text{ knife}}$
12. $\dfrac{4 \text{ pepperonis}}{3 \text{ olives}}$; $\dfrac{3 \text{ olives}}{4 \text{ pepperonis}}$

Lesson 6.2

1. True
2. False
3. True
4. False
5. True
6. False
7. True
8. True
9. $n = 60$
10. $x = 6$
11. $y = 39$
12. $m = 5$
13. $n = 27$
14. $x = 5$
15. $x = 29$
16. $n = 12$

Lesson 6.3

1. 12.8 teaspoons of sugar
2. 180 eggs
3. 15 quarts
4. 500 miles
5. T-Shirts: 12; Shorts: 9
6. 130 meals

Lesson 6.4

1. 20
2. 400
3. 40%
4. 10.2
5. 125
6. 6.6%
7. 49
8. 220
9. 2%
10. 133
11. 20
12. 37.5%

Lesson 6.5

1. $70.00
2. $43.75
3. $42.00
4. $72.00

Lesson 6.6

1. 30%
2. 17
3. 60%
4. 27
5. 12.5%
6. 25%
7. 9
8. 15%
9. 77
10. 120%
11. 26
12. 30%
13. 6%
14. 5%
15. 26

Lesson 6.7

1. 25%
2. 49.2%
3. 66%
4. 40%
5. 20%
6. $\dfrac{1}{5}$
7. $\dfrac{1}{6}$
8. $\dfrac{3}{8}$
9. $\dfrac{14}{25}$
10. $\dfrac{8}{25}$
11. 42%
12. 52.5%

Lesson 6.8

1. 76.12%
2. 1.543%
3. 159%
4. 57.21%
5. .12%
6. .0134%
7. 1045%
8. 189%
9. 56.9%
10. 99.99%
11. .11%
12. 313.45%
13. 9999%
14. 17.5555578%
15. 18.7%
16. 87%

Lesson 6.9

1. $600.00
2. $300.00
3. $540.00
4. $1,360.00

Lesson 6.9 (cont.)

5. $938.66
6. $595.56
7. $6871.95
8. 7 years at 12% balance: compound $1,105.34 vs $1,040.00 for simple

Answers

1. 49
2. 98
3. 157
4. 3027
5. 189
6. 2245
7. 280
8. 429
9. 124.6
10. 175.5
11. 349.5
12. 313.4
13. 375.8
14. 44.0
15. 567.0
16. 61.2
17. 1536.34
18. 32.46
19. 119.00
20. 523.76
21. 1099.99
22. 1.12
23. 33.44
24. 555.56
25. 729.240
26. 409.134
27. 8056.708
28. 549.595
29. 99.800
30. 177.556
31. 2012.205
32. 901.901

Lesson 7.2

1. 1.313
2. 2.571
3. .240
4. 3.750
5. .030
6. 7.394
7. .333
8. 4.733
9. 1.000
10. 2.423
11. 2.469
12. 2.592
13. 4.289
14. .944
15. 5.438
16. 4.684
17. 2.001
18. .028
19. 1.942
20. 3.636

Lesson 7.3

1. $\frac{13}{10}$
2. $\frac{3}{5}$
3. $\frac{147}{250}$
4. $\frac{31}{8}$
5. $\frac{27}{4}$
6. $\frac{9}{8}$
7. $\frac{163}{50}$
8. $\frac{5}{8}$
9. $\frac{21}{5}$
10. $\frac{12101}{1000}$
11. $\frac{2009}{1000}$
12. $\frac{5}{16}$
13. $\frac{67}{64}$
14. $\frac{66}{25}$
15. $\frac{111}{20}$
16. $\frac{11111}{500}$
17. $\frac{29}{5}$
18. $\frac{3399}{100}$
19. $\frac{7}{2}$
20. $\frac{409}{50}$
21. $\frac{5}{8}$
22. $\frac{3}{4}$

Lesson 7.4

1. .1332, 1.031, 1.3, 1.322, 1.5, 1.505, 1.55, 13.1
2. .075, .34, .705, .75, .751, 1.675, 1.68, 7.51
3. .00175, .01695, .017, .107, .17, 1.07, 1.7
4. .405, .415, .420, .45, .451, .625, 1.4
5. .333, .33, .25, .155, .15, .125
6. 1.001, .334, .3334, .332, .3033, .3, .0335
7. .751, .7501, .75, .707, .667, .6667, .6
8. .68, .6665, .63, .6, .59996, .55, .06665

Lesson 8.1

1. 167.9817
2. 838.131
3. 139.011543
4. 20.2349
5. 76.156
6. 24.31
7. 16.948
8. 46.4309
9. 10.3341
10. 37.618
11. 13.3031
12. 19.7103
13. 343.729
14. 65.1937
15. 12.16342
16. 3.9451
17. 34.2252 meters
18. 3.8463 inches

Lesson 8.2

1. 11.9375
2. 12.4382
3. 100.3899
4. 4.7797
5. 5.5563
6. 13.7372
7. 462.6875
8. 2.16069
9. .6683
10. 8.94666
11. 6.0655
12. .7491
13. 124.157
14. 2.7392
15. 1.971
16. 254.931
17. .384 meters
18. 8.0284 inches

Answers

Lesson 9.1

1. 478.17
2. 17.45458
3. 62.625
4. 11.9391
5. 598.29
6. 36.3
7. 145.6
8. 348.315
9. 15107.4
10. 844.8
11. 33.75
12. 12.88
13. 410.76
14. 5626.7379
15. 356.8992
16. 129.63104
17. 33.3 gallons
18. Yes, the total weight of the packages is 880.3328 pounds

Lesson 9.2

1. 74.279
2. 58.59
3. 27.756
4. 19.545
5. 64.595
6. 7.332
7. 9.483
8. 32.564
9. 68.704
10. 44.318
11. 8.446
12. 3.830

Lesson 10.1

1. 4^{10}
2. 7^2
3. 3^{12}
4. 12^{27}
5. 11^{12}
6. 12^{22}
7. 10^9
8. 23^1
9. 16^{14}
10. 15^2
11. 11^9
12. 4^{11}

Lesson 10.2

1. 5^{12}
2. 8^{35}
3. 14^{70}
4. 3^{160}
5. 7^{1296}
6. 8^{16}
7. 19^{512}
8. 15^{729}
9. 8^{24}
10. 2^{30}
11. 7^{60}
12. 13^{15}
13. 18^{256}
14. 277^{1296}
15. 33^{45}
16. 3^{20}

Lesson 10.3

1. $\dfrac{1}{64}$
2. $\dfrac{1}{27}$
3. $\dfrac{1}{1296}$
4. $\dfrac{1}{3125}$
5. $\dfrac{1}{49}$
6. $\dfrac{1}{4}$
7. $\dfrac{1}{59049}$
8. $\dfrac{1}{256}$
9. 8^{-2} or 2^{-6}
10. 9^{-2}
11. 3^{-2}
12. 5^{-2}
13. 16 or 4^2
14. 125 or 5^3
15. 117,649 or 7^6
16. 38,416 or 14^4

Lesson 10.4

1. 7
2. 11
3. 15
4. 9
5. 12
6. 2
7. 1
8. 13
9. 9 and 10; 9
10. 6 and 7; 7
11. 2 and 3; 2
12. 7 and 8; 7
13. 9 and 10; 10
14. 4 and 5; 5

Lesson 10.5

1. 1.3×10^{-3}
2. 8.10114×10^2
3. 4.0095×10^0
4. 5.0×10^{-5}
5. 5.851×10^{-1}
6. 2.20467×10^2
7. 4.267×10^2
8. 1.190155×10^4
9. 6.06544×10^{-2}
10. 8.852×10^{-1}
11. 1.488951×10^3
12. 2.0000199×10^5
13. 6.66×10^{-4}
14. 2.679×10^{-3}
15. 1.111×10^0
16. 3.0075×10^3
17. 266,990
18. 1,445.5
19. 9,660,317.1
20. 30,302
21. .00277
22. 391,918.1
23. 1,588
24. .010801

Lesson 11.1

1. 13
2. 0
3. 64
4. 45
5. 6
6. 11
7. 3
8. 21

Answers

Lesson 11.2

1. Commutative Property of Multiplication
2. Associative Property of Addition
3. Commutative Property of Multiplication
4. Commutative Property of Addition
5. Commutative Property of Addition
6. Associative Property of Addition
7. Associative Property of Addition
8. Commutative Property of Multiplication
9. Associative Property of Addition
10. Commutative Property of Multiplication
11. Commutative Property of Addition
12. Associative Property of Addition
13. Commutative Property of Addition
14. Commutative Property of Addition

Lesson 11.3

1. Zero Identity of Addition
2. Distributive Property
3. Zero Identity Property of Addition
4. Distributive Property
5. Distributive Property
6. Zero Identity of Addition
7. Distributive Property
8. Zero Identity of Addition
9. Distributive Property
10. Zero Identity of Addition
11. $4(5) + 4(7)$
12. $2(6 + 8)$

Lesson 11.4

1. 0
2. 0
3. 0
4. 0
5. Equality Property of Multiplication
6. Equality Property of Addition
7. Equality Property of Subtraction
8. Equality Property of Division
9. Equality Property of Division
10. Equality Property of Addition
11. Equality Property of Addition
12. Equality Property of Division

Lesson 12.1

1.
   F(−8.5); E(−8); G(−4.5); C(−2.5); A(−1); B(1); D(1.5)
2. 8, 4.6, 3.3, 3, −3, −3.3, −4.3, −6, −6.6, −6.7, −8.1
3. <
4. <
5. >
6. <
7. >
8. <
9. =
10. <
11. <

Lesson 12.2

1. 139
2. −84
3. −1
4. 399
5. 426
6. −181
7. −847
8. 28
9. 79
10. 65
11. 89
12. −20
13. −82
14. −169
15. 28
16. 12

Lesson 12.3

1. 15
2. −150
3. −8.33
4. 75
5. −225
6. −300
7. −28
8. −231
9. 225
10. −618
11. 14
12. 2420
13. 112
14. −3
15. 15
16. $\frac{1}{12}$
17. $-\frac{1}{18}$
18. 169

Lesson 13.1

1. A number divided by two, plus twenty-two
2. A number plus four
3. Four times a number plus three
4. A number times nine-tenths, minus nine
5. A number minus four divided by twenty
6. Three times a number plus seven, minus eight, plus thirty-three
7. Three times a number minus nine
8. Five divided by a number

Answers

Lesson 13.2

1. $x = 8$
2. $s = 9$
3. $z = 35$
4. $f = 3$
5. $m = 65$
6. $c = 44$
7. $y = 31$
8. $l = 90$
9. $k = 36$
10. $u = 15$
11. $t = 17$
12. $a = 9$
13. $b = 30$
14. $e = 32$
15. $d = 24$

Lesson 13.3

1. $n = 7$
2. $q = 45$
3. $f = 7$
4. $b = 3$
5. $k = 13$
6. $s = 5$
7. $m = 120$
8. $h = 7$
9. $x = 90$
10. $n = 14$
11. $m = 4$
12. $d = 13$

Lesson 13.4

1. $x = 3$
2. $x = 1$
3. $x = \dfrac{7}{4}$
4. $x = 15$
5. $x = \dfrac{2}{5}$
6. $z = 6$
7. $x = 8$
8. $r = 2$
9. $d = -\dfrac{2}{3}$
10. $b = \dfrac{4}{5}$
11. $q = -12$
12. $f = \dfrac{7}{3}$
13. $j = 7$
14. $r = 2$
15. $k = \dfrac{1}{9}$
16. $v = -\dfrac{5}{4}$

Lesson 14.1

1.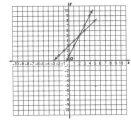

2. A(1,1); B(4,−4);
   C(−5,−9); D(9,5);
   E(2,6); F(−1,−2);
   G(−2,2); H(−6,4);
   I(1,7); J(−4,4)

3. A(1,3); B(2,5); C(3,7);
   D(4,9); E(3,−6);
   F(−1,−6); G(−4,4);
   H(−6,5); I(1,7);
   J(−3,3)

Lesson 14.2

1.

x	y
0	1
1	2
2	3
3	4
4	5
5	6

2.

x	y
−2	−2
−1	0
0	2
1	4
2	6
3	8

3.

x	y
0	−4
1	−3
4	0
6	2
8	4
10	6

4.

x	y
−1	−5
0	−3
1	−1
2	1
3	3
5	7

5.

x	y
−2	−3
1	3
0	1
2	5
4	9
6	13

6.

x	y
−4	−1
−2	0
0	1
2	2
4	3
6	4

7. $y = x + 2$
8. $y = 2x + 9$
9. $y = x^2 + 2$
10. $y = x^3$

Lesson 14.3

1. (2,5);

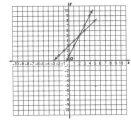

2. (3,−1);

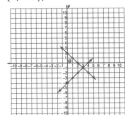

3. (1,1);

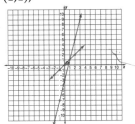

Answers

Lesson 15.1

1. 6 ft
2. 144 in.
3. 44 in.
4. 16 ft
5. 1.5 mi
6. $5\frac{1}{2}$ yd
7. 57 in.
8. .2 mi
9. 50688 in.
10. $5\frac{1}{2}$ ft
11. 18 yd
12. $22\frac{1}{2}$ ft = 270 in.
13. $11\frac{2}{3}$ yd
14. 600 in.
15. 11469 ft
16. 1248 in.
17. 72 sections
18. 49 yd; 147 ft

Lesson 15.2

1. 18 qt
2. 48 c
3. 14 c
4. 768 qt
5. 82 gal
6. 36 c
7. 25 c
8. 13 qt
9. 12 c
10. $8\frac{1}{4}$ gal
11. 18 c
12. $1\frac{7}{8}$ gal = 30 c
13. 8.9 gal
14. 16 gal
15. 66 pt = 33 qt
16. 274 pt
17. 24 gal 3 qt
18. 3 qt 3 c

Lesson 15.3

1. $5\frac{3}{8}$ lb
2. 133 oz
3. 20,000 lb
4. 1.2 T
5. $10\frac{3}{8}$ lb
6. 214 oz
7. 500 lb
8. 800 lb
9. 81 oz
10. 6.5 lb
11. $31\frac{1}{8}$ lb
12. 160 lb
13. 19 lb 11 oz
14. 65 lb 12 oz

Lesson 15.4

1. 20 in.
2. 26 in.
3. 108 in.
4. 44 in.
5. 17 in.
6. 36 ft
7. 81 ft

Lesson 15.5

1. 30 sq in.
2. 16 sq mi
3. 6 sq in.
4. 36 sq in.
5. 45 sq ft
6. 62.5 sq in.
7. 9 sq in.
8. 60 sq in.

Lesson 16.1

1. .21 km
2. 14.5 cm
3. 57300 cm
4. 26000 mm
5. .004 km
6. 40000 cm
7. 1600 mm
8. 2500 m
9. .116 m
10. 1,557,000 mm
11. 435.5 cm
12. 46670 cm
13. 3055.6 mm
14. 625 cm
15. 775 m

Lesson 16.2

1. .873 L
2. .001455 kL
3. 4750 mL
4. 7.945 L
5. .0001 kL
6. 2.554 L
7. 2.5 mL
8. 7000 mL
9. 340 times
10. 4.5 containers
11. 5.2126 L
12. 1756 mL

Lesson 16.3

1. .4 kg
2. 225,000,000 mg
3. 6.6 kg
4. 4.505 g
5. 21,350,000 mg
6. .53 g
7. .65 g
8. 7,100,000 cg
9. 3721 g
10. 2.313 kg
11. .546 g
12. 12.305 kg
13. 4.43 g
14. 12340 g
15. .000002 kg
16. 300,000,000 mg
17. 25.8 cg
18. .065 kg
19. 1.1394 g
20. The first hive; 18.315 grams

Lesson 16.4

1. 40 cm; 100 sq cm
2. 38 cm
3. 20.8 cm; 26.4 cm
4. 36 meters; 72 sq meters
5. 90 sq m
6. 24 sq m
7. $226.80
8. 14.4 m

Lesson 17.1

1. 35.56 cm
2. 4.575 m
3. 10.968 m
4. 3.656 m
5. 4.827 km
6. .948 L
7. 1.419 L
8. 8.514 L
9. 13.2475 L
10. 325.314 mL
11. 396.9 g
12. 1.362 kg
13. 170.1 g
14. 3218 m
15. 2.607 L
16. 4.8 lbs of silver
17. 36.6 meters
18. 7568 mL

Lesson 17.2

1. .936 in.
2. 56.342 in.
3. 118.11 in.
4. 2.484 mi
5. .7 oz
6. 6.342 qt
7. 792.6 gal
8. 9.9225 lb
9. 9.44 in.
10. 458.64 oz
11. 42.9 in.
12. 71.12 oz
13. The 6 ft 4 in. volleyball players are taller on average
14. 6.21 miles

Lesson 17.3

1. 302° F
2. 65.6° C
3. 32° F
4. −17.8° C
5. 102.2° C
6. 221° F
7. 22.2° C
8. 86° F
9. −31.7° C
10. 1.7° C
11. 98.6° F
12. 1742° F
13. 775° C
14. 100.4° F

Lesson 18.1

1. $\overset{\longleftrightarrow}{C \quad D}$
2. $\overset{\longleftrightarrow}{Q \quad R}$
3. Point D
4. $\overleftrightarrow{AB}, \overleftrightarrow{GH}, \overleftrightarrow{HG}, \overleftrightarrow{BA}$
5. A line drawn through point J and point K
6. C

Lesson 18.2

1. $\overset{\longrightarrow}{Y \quad X}$
2. $\overline{XZ}, \overline{ZX}, \overline{XY}, \overline{YX}, \overline{ZY},$ $\overline{YZ}, \overline{YM}, \overline{MY}, \overline{LY}, \overline{YL},$ $\overline{XL}, \overline{LX}, \overline{ZL}, \overline{LZ};$ Ray $\overrightarrow{XL}, \overrightarrow{ZL}, \overrightarrow{YL}, \overrightarrow{ML},$ $\overrightarrow{LM}, \overrightarrow{LX}, \overrightarrow{LZ}, \overrightarrow{LY}, \overrightarrow{XM},$ $\overrightarrow{XY}, \overrightarrow{XZ}, \overrightarrow{ZY}, \overrightarrow{ZM}, \overrightarrow{YM}$
3. $\overline{ED}, \overline{DE}, \overline{EA}, \overline{AE},$ $\overline{DC}, \overline{CD}, \overline{AB}, \overline{BA},$ $\overline{BC}, \overline{CB}$
4.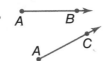
5. $\overline{CD}, \overline{NP}, \overline{PN}, \overline{DC}$

Lesson 19.1

1. Acute
2. Right
3. Acute
4. Obtuse
5. Acute
6. Obtuse
7. Right
8. Obtuse

Lesson 19.2

1. Complementary: ∠AGB; ∠BGC and ∠DGE; ∠EGF; Supplementary: ∠BGC and ∠BCF; ∠BGA and ∠AGE; ∠CGA and ∠FGA; ∠AGF and ∠FGD Vertical: ∠AGB and ∠DGE; ∠DGF and ∠AGC; ∠CGD and ∠AGF; ∠BGC and ∠FGE;
2. Complementary: ∠DFE and ∠DFC; ∠CFB and ∠BFA; Supplementary: ∠AFC and ∠CFE; ∠AFB and ∠BFE; ∠AFD and ∠DFE
3. Yes; sum of the angles = 90°
4. ∠a = ∠c = ∠g = ∠e
5. ∠a = 125°; ∠b = 55°; ∠c = 125°; ∠e = 125°; ∠f = 55°; ∠h = 55°

Lesson 19.3

1. ∠a = 108°, ∠b = 72°, ∠c = 108°, ∠d = 72°, ∠e = 108°, ∠f = 72°, ∠g = 108°
2. ∠1 = 48°; ∠2 = 132°; ∠3 = 48°; ∠4 = 132°; ∠5 = 48°; ∠6 = 132°; ∠7 = 48°; ∠8 = 132°
3. ∠a = 125°; ∠b = 55°; ∠c = 125°; ∠d = 55°; ∠e = 125°; ∠g = 125°; ∠h = 55°
4. ∠FOE = 46°, ∠EOC = 90°, ∠BOC = 44°

Lesson 20.1

1. Acute
2. Obtuse
3. Right
4. Obtuse
5. Right
6. Acute
7. Equilateral
8. Isosceles
9. Scalene

Lesson 20.2

1. Congruent: equal angles and sides
2. Neither: sides and angles are not equal
3. Similar: Equal angles but not sides
4. Similar: Proportionate sides
5. Similar: equal angles not sides
6. Congruent: equal angles and sides

Answers

Lesson 20.3

1. 10
2. $9\sqrt{2}$
3. 26
4. 12
5. 8
6. 13

Lesson 20.3 (cont.)

1. HI = 50 ft; KL = 30 ft; JL = 78 ft
2. LN = 25m; PQ = 21 m; OQ = 35 m
3. RT = $5\sqrt{2}$ in.; VW = 20 in.; UW = $20\sqrt{2}$ in.
4. 16 ft

Lesson 21.1

1. Square
2. Trapezoid
3. Rectangle
4. Rectangle
5. Trapezoid
6. Square
7. Rhombus
8. Kite
9. Rectangle

Lesson 21.2

1. Polygon
2. Not a polygon
3. Polygon
4. Polygon
5. Not a polygon
6. Polygon
7. Polygon
8. Polygon
9. Polygon

Lesson 21.3

1. 2 cm
2. 14 in.
3. 4 ft
4. d
5. 3 in.
6. $\overline{AO}, \overline{OB}$

Lesson 21.3 (cont.)

1. Area 100π, Circumference 20π
2. Circumference 14π, Radius 7
3. Diameter 10 cm; Area 25π sq cm; Circumference 10π cm
4. Circumference 12π cm; Area 36π sq cm
5. 100π inches or 314 in.
6. 10π km

Lesson 21.4

1. Translation
2. Rotation
3. Symmetry
4. Projection

Lesson 22.1

1. 96 sq cm
2. 160 sq in
3. 72 sq m
4. 56π sq in.
5. 440 sq cm
6. 114π sq in.

Lesson 22.2

1. 90π cu ft
2. 36 cu ft
3. 64 cu m
4. 432π cu in.
5. 140 cu cm
6. 16π cu ft

Lesson 22.2 (cont.)

1. 480 cu ft
2. 32π cu ft
3. 32 cu yd
4. 120π cu ft
5. 140 cu ft
6. 33π cu ft

Lesson 23.1

1. Red
2. April, May
3. Most: December; Least: July
4. Carl, Elaine
5. Drama
6. Most: Rapid Rail; Least: Motor Bus
7. The number of visitors grew from 1995–1997 then fell off 1998 and 1999

Lesson 23.2

1. June is the rainiest month
2. Wednesday, Saturday, Sunday
3. Friday, Saturday, Wednesday
4. David gets worse the later he plays in the day
5. The value of the car falls rapidly until 60,000 miles and then declines more moderately
6. Thursday

Answers

Lesson 23.3

1. Car A; the longer it goes the closer it gets to Taree

2. Town A

3. Internet use surpassed television use

4. People continue to move from the country to the cities.

Lesson 23.4

1. Housing, Transportation, and Other

2. Region 1 and Region 2, or Region 2 and Region 3

Lesson 24.1

1. Mean: 5; Median: 5; Range: 8; Mode: n/a

2. Mean: 35; Median: 17.5; Range: 100; Mode: 10

3. Mean: 26; Median: 24; Range: 55; Mode: 23

4. Mean: 35.6; Median: 27.5; Range: 66; Mode: 11

5. Mean: 4.4; Median: 3; Range: 5; Mode: 3

6. Mean: 14.6; Median: 15; Range: 23; Mode: 5, 21

7. Mean: 20.4; Median: 13; Range: 47; Mode: 9

8. Mean: 10; Median: 15; Range: 40; Mode: −10

9. Mean: 3.6; Median: −1; Range: 34; Mode: −1

10. Mean: 0; Median: 0; Range: 40; Mode: −20, 20

Lesson 24.2

1. 39, 40, 41, 45, 47, 47, 47, 49, 52, 56, 56, 56,

2. 120, 125, 128, 128, 130, 131, 132, 134, 136, 137, 139, 141, 142, 143, 145, 145, 149, 161, 165

3. Median 35.5, Range 80, Mode n/a

4. 0 | 4 8
   1 | 2 6
   2 | 1 1 3

Lesson 24.3

1. 70

2. 38

3.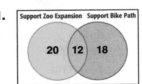

4. Range: 40; Median 76–77

Lesson 24.4

1. 12; 3

   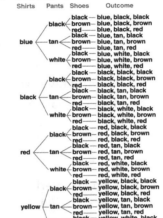

2. 36; 30; Fewer

Shirts	Pants	Shoes	Outcome

   blue — black — black — blue, black, black
   blue — black — brown — blue, black, brown
   blue — black — red — blue, black, red
   blue — tan — black — blue, tan, black
   blue — tan — brown — blue, tan, brown
   blue — tan — red — blue, tan, red
   blue — white — black — blue, white, black
   blue — white — brown — blue, white, brown
   blue — white — red — blue, white, red
   black — black — black — black, black, black
   black — black — brown — black, black, brown
   black — black — red — black, black, red
   black — tan — black — black, tan, black
   black — tan — brown — black, tan, brown
   black — tan — red — black, tan, red
   black — white — black — black, white, black
   black — white — brown — black, white, brown
   black — white — red — black, white, red
   red — black — black — red, black, black
   red — black — brown — red, black, brown
   red — black — red — red, black, red
   red — tan — black — red, tan, black
   red — tan — brown — red, tan, brown
   red — tan — red — red, tan, red
   red — white — black — red, white, black
   red — white — brown — red, white, brown
   red — white — red — red, white, red
   yellow — black — black — yellow, black, black
   yellow — black — brown — yellow, black, brown
   yellow — black — red — yellow, black, red
   yellow — tan — black — yellow, tan, black
   yellow — tan — brown — yellow, tan, brown
   yellow — tan — red — yellow, tan, red
   yellow — white — black — yellow, white, black
   yellow — white — brown — yellow, white, brown
   yellow — white — red — yellow, white, red

Lesson 24.5

1. 20 zoo only;
   18 bike path only

2. 20 jeans both;
   40 stone washed not boot cut; 60 boot cut not stone washed

Lesson 24.6

1. $\frac{7}{14}$ or $\frac{1}{2}$

2. $\frac{15}{35}$ or $\frac{3}{7}$

3. $\frac{212}{525}$

4. $\frac{3}{156}$ or $\frac{1}{52}$

Answers

1. 832 miles
2. 954 jeans
3. 108 m; $5\frac{2}{5}$ m
4. 5.5 oz or $\frac{11}{16}$ c
5. $8\frac{8}{15}$
6. −3
7. $x = 21$
8. $x = 6$
9. 80
10. $5^2 + 2^3 + 3^2 = 42$
11. 139.76 inches
12. 914.14 cm
13. Area: 96 sq cm; Perimeter: 40 cm; 15.748 in.
14. Area: 78.5 sq in; Circumference: 31.4 inches
15. Obtuse; Acute; Right;
16. Scalene; Equilateral; Isosceles
17. $23\frac{23}{25}$
18. 1
19. $\frac{3}{5}$
20. A(1,3); B(−3,6); C (2,−5), D(−2,−2)
21. 50 degrees
22. 1.566667
23. .1562
24. .31
25. 45%
26. $\frac{17}{4}$ or $4\frac{1}{4}$
27. 1.099, 1.161, 1.162, 1.90688, 1.9122, 2.163, 2.16302, 2.8022
28. 75
29. 2.4375
30. $67.50
31. $206.00; $212.00
32. Square; rectangle; rhombus; kite; trapezoid
33. $\frac{71}{13}$
34. $2\frac{11}{16}$
35. $\frac{3}{7}$
36. $2\frac{1}{5}$
37. 10^9
38. 9^4 or 6561
39. 144
40. 15
41. 47,50
42. Mango; strawberry
43. Molly; Megan
44. 12
45. 18
46. $x = 12$
47. Alternate interior angles: ∠4 and ∠5; ∠3 and ∠6; Alternate exterior angles: ∠2 and ∠7; ∠1 and ∠8; Vertical angles: ∠2 and∠3: ∠1 and ∠4; ∠6 and ∠7; ∠5 and ∠8; Supplementary angles: ∠1 and ∠3; ∠2 and ∠4; ∠6 and ∠8
48. Line segment $\overline{AB}$, $\overline{AC}$, $\overline{AF}$, $\overline{DB}$, $\overline{BE}$, $\overline{HG}$; rays: $\overrightarrow{AC}$, $\overrightarrow{AF}$, $\overrightarrow{BE}$, $\overrightarrow{BD}$; Line $\overleftrightarrow{AB}$
49. Volume = 72 cu in.; SA = 108 sq in.
50. Volume = 128π cu units; SA = 96π sq units
51. Volume = 96π

1. 1248 km
2. 1215 t-shirts
3. 81 meters; $13\frac{1}{2}$ meters
4. $37\frac{1}{3}$ cups
5. $11\frac{3}{8}$
6. −11
7. $x = 24$
8. $x = 8$
9. 66
10. $4^3 \times 3^2 + 5^2 = 601$
11. 183.1 inches
12. 1463 cm
13. 75 sq cm; 40 cm
14. 50.24 sq in.; 25.12 in.
15. Obtuse, acute, right
16. Scalene, equilateral, isosceles
17. 70
18. 1
19. $\frac{4}{65}$
20. A(1,3); B (−3,6); C (2,−5); D(−2,−2)
21. 27 degrees
22. 1.7
23. .18653
24. .2406
25. 36%
26. $\frac{45}{8}$; $5\frac{5}{8}$
27. 1.3561, 1.35688, 1.599, 2.356, 2.35692, 2.5622, 2.5631, 3.56302
28. 135
29. 2.28
30. $16.20
31. $512.50; $525.00
32. Square, rectangle, rhombus, kite, trapezoid
33. $\frac{63}{13}$
34. $5\frac{8}{13}$
35. $\frac{11}{7}$ or $1\frac{4}{7}$
36. 3
37. 10^9
38. 4^3
39. 225
40. 13
41. 57; 57
42. 20
43. Pineapple; Banana
44. Frank; Frank
45. 18
46. Alternate interior angles: ∠D and ∠F; ∠E and ∠C; Alternate exterior angles: ∠A and ∠G; ∠B and ∠H; Vertical angles: ∠A and ∠C; ∠B and ∠D; ∠E and ∠G; ∠F and ∠H; Supplementary angles: ∠A and ∠B; ∠B and ∠C; ∠A and ∠D; ∠E and ∠F; ∠F and ∠G; ∠G and ∠H; ∠H and ∠E; ∠H and ∠A; ∠G and ∠B; ∠E and ∠B; ∠F and ∠A; and others
47. 8
48. Line segments: $\overline{AB}$, $\overline{AF}$, $\overline{AC}$, $\overline{DB}$, $\overline{BE}$, $\overline{HG}$; Rays: $\overrightarrow{AF}$, $\overrightarrow{AC}$, $\overrightarrow{BE}$, $\overrightarrow{BD}$, $\overrightarrow{AB}$, $\overrightarrow{BA}$; Line $\overleftrightarrow{AB}$
49. Volume = 24 cu in; SA = 52 sq in.
50. Volume = 72π cu units; SA = 168π sq units
51. Volume = $\frac{40}{3}π$ cubic units

Answers

Unit Test Lesson 1-6

1. 90, 86
2. 41606
3. 236137
4. 1511691
5. 193
6. 1389
7. 120109
8. 91785
9. $8\frac{1}{2}$
10. $\frac{6}{43}$
11. 10
12. $3\frac{8}{39}$
13. $\frac{9}{61}$
14. $6\frac{3}{7}$
15. $8\frac{1}{4}$
16. 22
17. $5\frac{1}{2}$
18. $\frac{11}{36}$
19. $3\frac{1}{15}$
20. 14
21. $\frac{1}{87}$
22. $\frac{3}{47}$
23. 18

24. $\frac{4}{81}$
25. $\frac{5}{83}$
26. No
27. No
28. No
29. Yes
30. $x = 15$
31. $x = 50$
32. $x = 30$
33. $\frac{3}{4}$ grams
34. 20 miles
35. 33 batches
36. $2\frac{4}{9}$ qts
37. 4 times
38. $\frac{21}{50}$
39. 176
40. 12%
41. 28%
42. 127.5%
43. .3032
44. 1.601
45. 120%
46. $40, $50, $40
47. $4.77
48. $206.00, $212.00
49. $420.25; $452.56

Unit Test Lessons 7-9

1. 3407.0
2. 334,782.1
3. 65,529.1
4. 2,467,891.36
5. 97.01
6. 17.9999
7. 99.1112
8. ten thousandths
9. hundredths
10. $\frac{4}{5}$
11. $\frac{7}{8}$
12. $\frac{2}{25}$
13. .6
14. .5333
15. .1875
16. .1145, .122, .2126, .3132, .513, .616, .6165, .819
17. .0133, .0217, .0487, .05205, .05257, .1243, .20413, .217, .5257
18. 3.472817
19. 6.53518656
20. 6.660933
21. 1.91916
22. 1.428711
23. 2.24946656
24. $6.75

25. $2.78
26. 36.297
27. 2119.175
28. $0.11
29. 7.48935
30. 91.84
31. 2.9768005
32. $2.36
33. 1.478625
34. 6.381
35. 11.70
36. 23.22
37. .383135
38. 234.225
39. $0.25
40. 6.65405
41. $1.03
42. 63.65 pounds
43. $33.30; Yes; $1.70
44. 12.925 miles
45. 17 pots
46. $99.11
47. 39.8 gallons

Answers

Unit Test Lessons 10-12

1. $4^3 + 3^3 = 91$
2. $3^2 \times 2^2 - 3^3 = 9$
3. $4^3 \times 2^2 + 4^2 + 6^2 - 3^2$ $= 299$
4. 1.3224714066×10^7
5. 2.5354011×10^4
6. 1.80705×10^{-1}
7. $2.22946981717 \times 10^{10}$
8. 8.660506×10^2
9. 1.186591×10^2
10. 72
11. 30
12. 50
13. 51
14. 64
15. 216
16. 4
17. 100
18. 1
19. 8
20. 12
21. 25
22. 14
23. 1.5
24. 1.3
25. 90
26. Identity Property of Multiplication
27. Identity Property of Addition
28. Associative Property of Addition
29. Distributive Property
30. Commutative Property of Addition
31. Equality Property of Subtraction
32. Zero Property of Multiplication
33. Equality Property of Addition
34. -5 – Point A
35. -7 – Point B
36. -8 – Point D
37. -3 – Point C
38. -1500
39. -9
40. 18
41. -9
42. 12
43. -60
44. -36
45. -5
46. -8

Unit Test Lesson 13-14

1. Two times a number plus fifteen
2. A number times five less twelve
3. $x = 3$
4. $x = 116$
5. $x = 5$
6. $x = 5$
7. $x = 10$
8. $x = 16$
9. $x = 15$
10. $x = 14$
11. $y = 4$
12. $y = 4$
13. $y = 4$
14. $y = 8$
15. $y = 4$
16. $y = 6$
17. $y = 2$
18. $y = 6$
19. A(1,1)
20. B(3,1)
21. C(−1,−3)
22. D(−1,2)
23. E(−2,1)
24. F(−3,−3)
25. G(4,−4)
26. H(5,5)

27.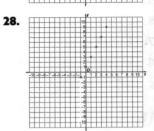

28.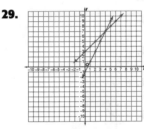

29.

Answer (4,7)

Answers

Unit Test Lessons 15-17

1. 1890 in.
2. 158 containers full
3. The second box $13\frac{3}{8}$ lb vs. 12.25 lb
4. 55 square meters
5. Area 132 sq ft, Perimeter 46 ft
6. Area 54 sq ft, Perimeter 432 inches
7. 7.5 sq ft
8. 1446 km, 86,760 km 2,082,240 km
9. 101,750 sq cm
10. 7.013 liters
11. 24 sq cm; 30 cm
12. 382 meters; 8190 sq m
13. 25.3 sq m
14. 75 kg
15. About 100 quarts, 25 gallons
16. 2700 sq ft; about 250 sq meters
17. About $2\frac{1}{2}$ hours
18. 71.6° to 82.4° F
19. 32 sq m
20. 48 sq in.
21. 16,500 ft
22. 39.8° C

Unit Tests Lesson 18-22

1. Obtuse
2. Right
3. Acute
4. Complementary; angle measurements add to 90°
5. Supplementary add to 180°
6. Complementary add to 90°
7. Equilateral
8. Isosceles
9. Equilateral
10. Right
11. Obtuse
12. Acute
13. Acute
14. Rectangle
15. Octagon
16. Rhombus
17. Trapezoid
18. Kite
19. Cube; Volume: 216 cu cm; SA: 216 sq cm
20. Rectangular solid; Volume: 840 cu cm; SA: 596 sq cm
21. Cone; Volume: 12π cu ft
22. Cylinder; Volume: 96π cu yd; SA: 80π sq yd
23. Point A
24. $\overline{CD}$, $\overline{BD}$, $\overline{BC}$
25. $\overline{HG}$
26. $\overline{AG}$, $\overline{AD}$, $\overline{AH}$
27. 25.12
28. 50.24
29. 128 sq cm
30. Yes
31. Yes
32. No
33. ∠2 and ∠3; No, sides are not equal
34. ∠1 and ∠3;
    ∠2 and ∠4;
    ∠5 and ∠7;
    ∠6 and ∠8, yes;
    Supplementary:
    ∠1 and ∠2;
    ∠2 and ∠3;
    ∠3 and ∠4;
    ∠1 and ∠4;
    ∠5 and ∠6;
    ∠6 and ∠7;
    ∠7 and ∠8;
    ∠8 and ∠5;
    Exterior angle pair:
    ∠1 and ∠7;
    ∠2 and ∠8;
    ∠8 and ∠5;
    Interior Angle Pair:
    ∠3 and ∠5;
    ∠4 and ∠6
35. △DEF, △GHI

Unit Test Lessons 23-24

1. $\frac{6}{12}$ or $\frac{1}{2}$; $\frac{1}{6}$; $\frac{5}{12}$; $\frac{1}{6}$
2. 49; 67; 67.5
3. 27; 9; 3
4. Median 6, range 1.5
5. Broccoli; Hummus; 7
6. July; September; July–August
7. 12 speed; 3 speed
8. June; 5
9.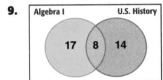